In God We Trust . . . Or Do We?

In God We Trust . . . Or Do We?

Our Nation Built on a Christian Foundation

Dr. Glover Shipp

RESOURCE *Publications* · Eugene, Oregon

IN GOD WE TRUST . . . OR DO WE?
Our Nation Built on a Christian Foundation

Copyright © 2011 Glover Shipp. All rights reserved. Except for brief quotations in critical publications or reviews, no part of this book may be reproduced in any manner without prior written permission from the publisher. Write: Permissions, Wipf and Stock Publishers, 199 W. 8th Ave., Suite 3, Eugene, OR 97401.

All Bible quotes are from the New International Version.

Resource Publications
An Imprint of Wipf and Stock Publishers
199 W. 8th Ave., Suite 3
Eugene, OR 97401

www.wipfandstock.com

ISBN 13: 978-1-61097-430-1

Manufactured in the U.S.A.

Contents

Acknowledgments / vii
Introduction / ix

Chapter 1. The Mayflower Compact (the Mother Document) and Other Papers from the Colonial Period / 1

Chapter 2. Colonial Organization and Charters / 7

Chapter 3. Other Documents Related to Revolution and Independence / 14

Chapter 4. The Declaration of Independence / 22

Chapter 5. Articles of Confederation and the Constitution / 27

Chapter 6. Constitutions of the Fifty States / 30

Chapter 7. Other Post-Revolution Documents / 37

Chapter 8. Lincoln's Addresses / 60

Chapter 9. More Recent Presidential Addresses that Refer to God / 63

Chapter 10. State of the Union Addresses and Reliance on God / 73

Chapter 11. The View of Congress on Government and Religion / 80

Chapter 12. The Supreme Court on our Religious Heritage as a Nation / 83

Chapter 13. References to God on our National Seal and Monuments / 95

Chapter 14. God in Our Pledge of Allegiance and Oaths of Office / 106

Chapter 15. God in Our National Anthem and Hymns / 109

Chapter 16. References to God in Poetry by Famous (and One Not Famous) Americans / 117

Chapter 17. Quotes from Famous Americans on God and the Bible / 127

Chapter 18. Current Voices on Faith in God / 138

Chapter 19. The High Cost of Liberty / 142

Chapter 20. Guarantee of Religious Freedom / 145

Chapter 21. Conclusion: In God We Trust . . . or Do We? / 150

Retrospect and Final Word: In God Do We Really Trust(?) / 157

Appendix: Were Our Founding Fathers Deists? / 159

Bibliography / 163

Acknowledgments

I AM indebted to my own parents and grandparents, as well as teachers, who instilled within me a strong sense of faith in God and loyalty toward our nation. My gratitude is profound for those who went before and paved the way to freedom with their blood. I am also indebted to Wipf and Stock Publishers for giving me the opportunity to publish through its network and to Christian Amondson, Assistant Managing Editor of Wipf & Stock, for his patience in helping see this book through the publishing process.

Introduction

In our age of inclusiveness and political correctness one being is being steadily expunged from our national documents, monuments, currency and other official items. That being is God.

In great part, our nation was first colonized and established by people of faith—not any faith, but faith in God. This doesn't mean that all were devout Christians, but it does mean that they recognized, in their endeavors to build a new society and government on this continent, that the difficulties they faced were too enormous to surmount without divine aid. As many as nine of the original thirteen colonies were settled to a considerable extent by those seeking religious liberty.

It is no wonder, then, that both colonial and all state charters included statements about reliance on God and/or a deep concern for Christian liberty. In addition, our own Declaration of Independence and Federal Constitution place the Lord as the eternal foundation for our government. In addition, every single one of the fifty state charters refers to God in its preamble.

Our Founding Fathers made statements to this same effect and they saw to it that references to God be included in officials documents, in oaths of office and on national monuments.

This same sense of reliance on God is seen in our National Anthem and other patriotic songs. It is seen in poems eulogizing our great nation.

It is with a profound sense of concern over our national loss of memory over the spiritual foundation for our nation, as well as over very dedicated efforts on the part of some individuals and groups to expunge God from our national documents and memory, that I purposed to write this book. In reading it, let the image of our national slogan, *"In God We Trust,"* be engraved on your heart. Let our forefathers' reliance on Divine Providence become yours. Let these quotations sink into your heart and grow a new and stronger reliance on God in it. Listen to what God revealed to ancient scribes in the Bible:

> *"If my people, who are called by my name, will humble themselves and pray and seek my face and turn from their wicked ways, then I will hear from heaven and will forgive their sin and will heal their land"* (2 Chron 7:14).

> *". . . Blessed are the people whose God is the Lord"* (Psalm 144:15).

And now from more contemporary writers:

> *"God who gave us life gave us liberty. And can the liberties of a nation be thought secure when we have removed their only firm basis, a conviction in the minds of the people that these liberties are a gift from God? That they are not to be violated but with His wrath? Indeed I tremble for my country*

when I reflect that God is just, and that His justice cannot sleep forever."[1]

"If we ever forget that we are One Nation *Under God*, then we will be a nation *gone under* . . . "[2]

My great fear is that we are no longer building a nation under god. We appear to be building yet one more monument—a national monument to failure. If faith in God does not underlie our national purpose, then we will certainly fail.

But you ask, *"Doesn't our Constitution prohibit the joining of church and state?"* No, all it says (found in the First Amendment) is that *Congress shall make no laws concerning the establishment of religion nor prohibiting the free exercise thereof.* This amendment, however, has been turned on its head. Now it reads, *"The people shall not have the right to pray or invoke God's name on public property or to make any reference to Him on public monuments."*

How did this come about? Concerted pressure by a small number of special-interest groups, joined with a compliant judicial system that has wrongly interpreted the First Amendment to prohibit much of the free exercise of religion guaranteed by the Constitution. As a result, both government and individuals are intimidated into backing away from any connection with God.

Yet, government still invokes God. Are you aware that congress has paid chaplains or that its sessions and those

---

1. Thomas Jefferson, *Jefferson Writings*, 1781, 4:289.
2. Ronald Reagan. Reunion Arena. Dallas, 1984. Recorded on www.themoralliberal.com/.ronald-reagan-on-if-we-forget-that-we-are-one-nation-under-god.

of the Supreme Court open with prayer? What is going on here? Isn't such behavior hypocritical? Or is it that, *"What is sauce for the goose is not legal for the gander?"*

Now let us take a look at our historical documents, monuments and other symbols of government that refer to God. The mentality of some seems to be that if we can expunge or at least ignore these references, they will go away. No, they won't. They are here for us to examine and learn from them.

Chapter 1

The Mayflower Compact (the Mother Document) and Other Papers from the Colonial Period

THE DATE was November 11, 1620. In preparation for launching their colony in the New World, the Pilgrim Fathers drew up a significant document that honored God and the Christian faith. Here it is, in its entirety:

> *"In the name of God, Amen. We, whose names are underwritten, the Loyal Subjects of our dread Sovereign Lord, King James, by the Grace of God, of England, France and Ireland, King, Defender of the Faith, e&. Having undertaken for the Glory of God, and Advancement of the Christian Faith, and the Honour of our King and Country, a voyage to plant the first colony in the northern parts of Virginia; do by these presents, solemnly and mutually in the Presence of God and one of another, covenant and combine ourselves together into a civil Body Politick, for our better Ordering and Preservation, and Furtherance of the Ends aforesaid; And by Virtue hereof to enact, constitute, and frame, such just and equal Laws, Ordinances, Acts, Constitutions and Offices, from time to time, as shall be thought most meet and convenient*

> *for the General good of the Colony; unto which we promise all due submission and obedience. In Witness whereof we have hereunto subscribed our names at Cape Cod the eleventh of November, in the Reign of our Sovereign Lord, King James of England, France and Ireland, the eighteenth, and of Scotland the fifty-fourth. Anno Domini, 1620."*

Did you notice the words that emphasize the Spiritual realm?

- In the name of God
- By the grace of God
- Glory of God
- Advancement of the Christian Faith
- The presence of God
- *Anno Domini* (in the year of our Lord)

Were the framers of this first formal document believers? Did they seek God's guidance? Certainly, on both questions. It is pointless to deny this.

GOVERNOR WILLIAM BRADFORD'S ACCOUNT OF RESCUE FROM STARVATION (ABOUT 1630)

"... for food (for the colonists) they were all alike ... The best dish they could present their friends with was a lobster or a piece of cold fish without bread or anything else but a cup of fair spring water ... but God game them health and strength in a good measure, and showed them by experience the truth of that word, (Deuteronomy viii:3) 'That man liveth

not by bread only, but by every word that proceedeth out of the mouth of Lord doth a man live.'

"I may not omit how, notwithstanding all their great pains and industry, and the great hopes of a large crop, the Lord seemed to blast . . . and to threaten further and more sore famine unto the . . . Upon which they set apart a solemn day of humiliation, to seek the Lord by humble and fervent prayer, in this great distress. And He was pleased to give them a gracious and speedy answer (rain)."

JOHN COTTON'S ANALYSIS OF THE BEST FORM OF GOVERNMENT, 1663

"To make the Lord God our Governor is the best form of government in a Christian Commonwealth . . . that form of government where (1) the people that have the power of choosing their governors are in covenant with God; (2) whereas the men chosen by them are godly men, and fitted with a spirit of government; (3) in which the laws they rule by are the laws of God; 4) wherein laws executed, inheritances allotted, and civil differences are composed, according to God's appointment . . ."

RULES FOR HARVARD, THE FIRST AMERICAN COLLEGE, 1636

"Let every student be plainly instructed; and earnestly pressed to consider well, the maine end of his life and studies is, to know God and Jesus Christ which is eternal life (John 17:3) and therefore to lay Christ in the bottom, as the only foundation of sound knowledge and Learning."

4 IN GOD WE TRUST ... OR DO WE?

RULES FOR YALE, 1787 STUDENT GUIDELINES

"All the scholars are required to live a religious and blameless life according to the rules of God's Word, diligently reading the Holy Scriptures, that fountain of Divine light and truth, and constantly attending all the duties of religion."

PUNISHMENT FOR MISSING WORSHIP, 1666

At a county court at Cambridge: *"Thomas Goold, Thomas Osburne and John George being presented by the grand jury of this county for absenting themselves from the publick worship of God on the Lords dayes for one whole yeare now past . . . The court sentenced the said Thomas Goold, Thomas Osburne and John George, for their absenting themselves from the publique worship of God on the Lords dayes, to pay four pounds fine."*

DIARY OF CHIEF JUSTICE SAMUEL SEWALL, 1692

"I prayed that God would pardon all my sinfull Wanderings, and direct me for the future. That God would bless the Assembly in their debates, and that would chuse and assist our Judges, etc., and save New England as to Enemies and Witchcrafts . . ."

THE STATE OF RELIGION IN THE JERSEYS, LEWIS MORRIS, 1700

"Middletown . . . is a large Township, there is no such thing as Church or Religion amongst them, they are p'haps the most ignorant and wicked People in the world, their meetings on

Sundays is [are] at the Public house, where they get their fill of Rum, and go to fighting and running of races . . ."

SHIPPED BY THE GRACE OF GOD, 1754

"Shipped by the grace of God, in good order and well-conditioned, by William Johnston & Co., owners of he schooner Sierra Leone . . . whereof is master under God for this present voyage, David Lindsay, and now riding at anchor in harbour of Newport, and by God's grace bound for the coast of Africa . . ."

THE SACRED RIGHTS OF MANKIND, ALEXANDER HAMILTON, 1774

"The Sacred Rights of Mankind are not be to rummaged for among old parchments or musty records. They are written, as with a sunbeam, in the whole volume of human nature, by the Hand of the Divinity itself, and can never be erased or obscured by moral power.

CONCLUSION

Our colonial pioneers faced untold hardships in their Atlantic crossing, getting a toehold in this new and promising land, fighting hostile Indians and severe weather conditions, succumbing to fatal illnesses and scratching out their first crops. For the most part, they appear to have realized that the task and dangers were too great to rely on themselves, so they invoked the Higher Power to aid them in their new start in a new land. Praise God for them and their faith and perseverance. I can trace my ancestry back to them and on to Scotland and England, principally. Where would I be today without their faith in the midst of struggle? And where would you be, if you are one of their descendants?

Chapter 2

Colonial Organization and Charters

THE ORIGINAL colonies, out of which came our nation, were formed for a variety of reasons. In some cases the reasons were religiously motivated, in other cases commercially motivated, and in some cases, both. Here is a list of these colonies in historical order and their motivation for being developed. The royal colony status of some colonies meant that they became officially owned and controlled by the British crown.

- **Virginia, 1607**, founded by the London Company primarily for commercial purposes. Became a royal colony in 1624.
- **Massachusetts, 1620**. Founded by Puritans primarily motivated by a desire for religious freedom. Became a royal colony in 1691.
- **New Hampshire, 1623**. Founded by John Wheelwright in part to provide a safe haven for religious dissidents. Became a royal colony in 1679.
- **Maryland, 1634**. Founded by Lord Baltimore for the most part to provide a homeland for Catholics.
- **Connecticut, c 1635**. Established by Thomas Hooker, primarily for religious reasons.

- **Rhode Island, 1636.** Founded by Roger Williams as a safe haven for religious dissidents.
- **Delaware, 1638.** Founded by Peter Minuit and New Sweden Company, in part due to religious motives.
- **North Carolina, 1653.** Founded by a group of Virginians. Became a royal colony in 1729. Religious motives were involved in its formation.
- **South Carolina, 1663.** Founded by eight British nobles granted as a charter by King Charles II. Became a royal colony in 1729.
- **New Jersey, 1664.** Founded by Lord Berkeley and Sir George Carteret, in part for religious reasons. Became a royal colony in 1702.
- **New York, 1664.** Founded by the Duke of York. Became a royal colony in 1685.
- **Pennsylvania, 1682.** Founded by William Penn as a refuge for Quakers.
- **Georgia, 1732.** Founded by James Edward Oglethorpe. Became a royal colony in 1752.

VIRGINIA, 1607

"We, greatly commending, and graciously accepting of, their Desires for the Furtherance of so noble a Work, which may, by the Providence of Almighty God, hereafter tend to the Glory of his Divine Majesty, in propagating of Christian Religion to such People, as yet live in Darkness and miserable Ignorance of the true Knowledge and Worship of God, and may in time bring the Infidels and Savages, living in those parts, to human

Civility, and to a settled and quiet Government: DO, by these our Letters Patents, graciously accept of, and agree to, their humble and well-intended Desires . . ."

MASSACHUSETTS, 1629

The most important work in the colony was building churches and establishing religious instruction. The minister was the most important man in the colony. No person was allowed to vote unless he was a member of the church. A reproof in church was considered the most disgraceful penalty that could be visited upon an individual.

MARYLAND, 1632

Aside from the fact that Maryland was the first of the proprietary governments, the colony is especially remembered in American history as the first to guarantee religious liberty. Lord Baltimore (Sir George Calvert), as an adherent of the Catholic faith, could not exclude his fellow-Catholics from his new colony. Such a course would have proved him untrue to his own principles and defeated one of his purposes in founding the colony—to furnish a home for oppressed Catholics who were shamefully treated in England at that time.

It was equally impossible for him to have excluded Protestants, being the subject of a Protestant king who ruled over a Protestant nation. Had he done this, he would have raised a storm in England, which would have been fatal to his colony. Therefore, he did the only wise thing to be done—he left the matter open to individual conscience.

RHODE ISLAND, 1663

Rhode Island was first settled by Roger Williams, who sought a place in which religious liberty would be guaranteed. After a period of dispute and unrest, Dr. John Clarke was commissioned to secure a document from the new British king, Charles II, that would both be consistent with the religious principles upon which the tiny colony was founded and also safeguard Rhode Island lands from encroachment by speculators and greedy neighbors. He succeeded admirably. The charter of 1663 guaranteed complete religious liberty, established a self-governing colony and strengthened Rhode Island's claims. It was the most liberal such document to be issued by Britain during the colonial era, a fact that enabled it to serve as Rhode Island's basic law until May 1843.

DELAWARE COLONIAL CHARTER, 1701

"Because no People can be truly happy, though under the greatest Enjoyment of Civil Liberties, if abridged of the Freedom of their Consciences, as to their Religious Profession and Worship: And Almighty God being the only Lord of Conscience, Father of Lights and Spirits; and the Author as well as Object of all divine Knowledge, Faith and Worship, who only doth enlighten the Minds, and persuade and convince the Understandings of People, I do hereby grant and declare, That no Person or Persons, inhabiting in this Province or Territories, who shall confess and acknowledge One almighty God, the Creator, Upholder and Ruler of the World; and professes him or themselves obliged to live quietly

under the Civil Government, shall be in any Case molested or prejudiced, in his or their Person or Estate, because of his or their conscientious Persuasion or Practice, nor be compelled to frequent or maintain any religious Worship, Place or Ministry, contrary to his or their Mind, or to do or suffer any other Act or Thing, contrary to their religious Persuasion.

"And that all Persons who also profess to believe in Jesus Christ, the Saviour of the World, shall be capable (notwithstanding their other Persuasions and Practices in Point of Conscience and Religion) to serve this Government in any Capacity, both legislatively and executively, he or they solemnly promising, when lawfully required, Allegiance to the King as Sovereign, and Fidelity to the Proprietary and Governor, and taking the Attests as now established by the Law made at Newcastle, in the Year One Thousand and Seven Hundred, entitled, An Act directing the Attests of several Officers and Ministers, as now amended and confirmed this present Assembly."

NORTH CAROLINA, 1663

Prospective colonists were guaranteed "all liberties, franchises and privileges of this our kingdom of England" and be able to "possess and enjoy" them "without the least molestation, vexation, trouble or grievance." Religious toleration was to be granted to those "Who really in their Judgments, and for Conscience sake" could not conform to the ritual and beliefs of the established Church of England."

SOUTH CAROLINA, 1629

"We therefore tendering the good and happy Success of the said Plantation, both in Regard of the General Weal of human Society, as in Respect of the Good of our own Estate and Kingdoms, and being willing to give Furtherance unto all good Means that may advance the Benefit of the said Company, and which may secure the Safety of our loving Subjects planted in our said Colony, under the Favour and Protection of God Almighty . . . "[1]

NEW JERSEY

Charter or Fundamental Laws, of West New Jersey, 1676
Chapter XVI

"That no men, nor number of men upon earth, hath power or authority to rule over men's consciences in religious matters, therefore it is consented, agreed and ordained, that no person or persons whatsoever within the said Province, at any time or times hereafter, shall be any ways upon any presence whatsoever, called in question, or in the least punished or hurt, either in person, estate, or privilege, for the sake of his opinion, judgment, faith or worship towards God in matters of religion. But that all and every such person, and persons may from time to time, and at all times, freely and fully have, and enjoy his and their judgments, and the exercises of their consciences in matters of religious worship throughout all the said Province."

---

1. Charter issued by King James I.

PENNSYLVANIA

Charter for the Province of Pennsylvania, 1681

"Charles the Second by the Grace of God King of England, Scotland, France and Ireland Defender of the Faith &c To our Right Trusty and Well beloved Chancellor Heneage Lord Finch our Chancellor of England greeting Wee will and command you that under our Great Seale of England remaining in your Custody you cause our Letters to be made Forth patents in form following:

"And Our further pleasure is and wee doe hereby, for us, our heires and Successors, charge and require, that if any of the inhabitants of the said Province, to the number of Twenty, shall at any time hereafter be desirous, and shall by any writing, or by any person deputed for them, signify such their desire to the Bishop of London for the time being that any preacher or preachers, to be approved of by the said Bishop, may be sent unto them for their instruction, that then such preacher or preachers shall and may be and reside within the said Province, without any denial or molestation whatsoever."

CONCLUSION

What do we see in these colonial charters? Throughout them there is a thread of acknowledgment that God is Sovereign and that he rules over the colonies. There is also a thread of guaranteed religious liberty, permitting each citizen to worship according to the dictates of his or her own conscience. There is even a thread in the Pennsylvania Charter providing support for preachers to instruct the people.

Chapter 3

Other Documents Related to Revolution and Independence

THERE ARE many extant documents from before, during and immediately following the Revolutionary War that invoke God. Following are excerpts from some of these:

SATISFACTION IN GOD

"Our continual apprehension of God, may produce our continual satisfaction in God, under all His dispensations. Whatever enjoyments are by God conferred upon us, where lies the relish, where the sweetness of them? Truly, we may come to relish our enjoyments, only so far as we have something of God in them. It was required in Psalm xxxvii. 4, 'Delight thyself in the Lord.' Yea, and what if we should have no delight but the Lord? Let us ponder with ourselves over our enjoyments: 'In these enjoyments I see God, and by these enjoyments, I serve God!'

"And now, let all our delight in, and all our value and fondness for our enjoyments, be only, or mainly, upon such a divine score as this. As far as any of our enjoyments lead us unto God, so far let us relish it, affect it, embrace it, and rejoyce in it: 'O taste, and feed upon God in all;' and ask for

nothing, no, not for life itself, any further than as it may help us, in our seeing and our serving of our God.

"And then, whatever afflictions do lay fetters upon us, let us not only remember that we are concerned with God therein, but let our concernment with God procure a very profound submission in our souls. Be able to say with him in Psalm xxxix. 9, 'I open not my mouth, because thou didst it.' In all our afflictions, let us remark the justice of that God, before whom, 'why should a living man complain for the punishment of his sin?' The wisdom of that God, 'whose judgments are right:' the goodness of that God, who 'punishes us less than our iniquities do deserve.' Let us behave ourselves, as having to do with none but God in our afflictions: And let our afflictions make us more conformable unto God: which conformity being effected, let us then say, 'Tis good for me that I have been afflicted.'

"Sirs, what were this, but a pitch of holiness, almost angelical! Oh! Mount up, as with the wings of eagles, of angels: be not a sorry, puny, mechanick sort of Christians any longer; but reach forth unto these things that are thus before you."

GIVE ME LIBERTY OR GIVE ME DEATH

Patrick Henry, March 23, 1775, before the Virginia House of Burgesses:

"No man thinks more highly than I do of the patriotism, as well as abilities, of the very worthy gentlemen who have just addressed the House. But different men often see the same subject in different lights; and, therefore, I hope it will not be thought disrespectful to those gentlemen if, entertaining as I do opinions of a character very opposite to theirs, I

shall speak forth my sentiments freely and without reserve. This is no time for ceremony. The question before the House is one of awful moment to this country. For my own part, I consider it as nothing less than a question of freedom or slavery; and in proportion to the magnitude of the subject ought to be the freedom of the debate. It is only in this way that we can hope to arrive at truth, and fulfill the great responsibility which we hold to God and our country. Should I keep back my opinions at such a time, through fear of giving offense, I should consider myself as guilty of treason towards my country, and of an act of disloyalty toward the Majesty of Heaven, which I revere above all earthly kings . . .

"*They tell us, sir, that we are weak; unable to cope with so formidable an adversary. But when shall we be stronger? Will it be the next week, or the next year? Will it be when we are totally disarmed, and when a British guard shall be stationed in every house? Shall we gather strength by irresolution and inaction? Shall we acquire the means of effectual resistance by lying supinely on our backs and hugging the delusive phantom of hope, until our enemies shall have bound us hand and foot? Sir, we are not weak if we make a proper use of those means which the God of nature hath placed in our power. The millions of people, armed in the holy cause of liberty, and in such a country as that which we possess, are invincible by any force which our enemy can send against us. Besides, sir, we shall not fight our battles alone. There is a just God who presides over the destinies of nations, and who will raise up friends to fight our battles for us. The battle, sir, is not to the strong alone; it is to the vigilant, the active, the brave. Besides, sir, we have no election. If we were base enough to desire it, it is now too late to retire from the contest. There is no* retreat but in submission and slavery! Our chains are forged! Their clanking may be heard on the plains of Boston! The war is inevitable—and let it come! I repeat it, sir, let it come.

"It is in vain, sir, to extenuate the matter. Gentlemen may cry, Peace, Peace—but there is no peace. The war is actually begun! The next gale that sweeps from the north will bring to our ears the clash of resounding arms! Our brethren are already in the field! Why stand we here idle? What is it that gentlemen wish? What would they have? Is life so dear, or peace so sweet, as to be purchased at the price of chains and slavery? Forbid it, Almighty God! I know not what course others may take; but as for me, give me liberty or give me death!"

PATRICK HENRY ON THE TRUE PILLARS OF GOVERNMENT

"The great pillars of all government and social life [are] virtue, morality and religion . . . If we loose these we are conquered indeed."

THE NECESSITY FOR TAKING UP ARMS, JOHN HANCOCK, 1775

"With an humble confidence in the mercies of the supreme and impartial Judge and Ruler of the universe, we most devoutly implore his divine goodness to protect us happily through this great conflict . . ." (By order of Congress).

SAMUEL LANGDON, PRESIDENT OF HARVARD

In an address to the Provincial Congress of Massachusetts, May 31, 1775, *"If God be for us, who can be against us? The enemy [the British Army] has reproached us for calling on His name and professing our trust in Him . . ."*

WILLIAM PENN

"For my country, I eyed the Lord in the obtaining of it, and the more I was drawn inward to look to Him and owe it to His hand and power, than to any other way."

DANIEL WEBSTER

"Our ancestors established their system of government on morality and religious sentiment . . . Whatever makes a man a good Christian also makes a good citizen."

JOHN JAY, FIRST SUPREME COURT JUSTICE

"Americans should select and prefer Christians as their rulers."

JACOB DUCHE, MEMBER OF THE CONTINENTAL CONGRESS, FIRST PRAYER OFFERED IN CONGRESS, 1774

"Be thou present, O God of Wisdom, and direct the councils of this honorable assembly; enable them to settle things on the best and surest foundation. That the scene of blood may be speedily closed; that order, harmony, and peace may be restored, and truth and justice, religion and piety, prevail

and flourish amongst the people. Preserve the health of their bodies and vigor of their minds; shower down on them and the millions they here represent, such temporal blessings as Thou seest expedient for them in this world and crown them with glory in the world to come. All this we ask in the name and through the merits of Jesus Christ, Thy Son and our Savior. Amen."

GEORGE WASHINGTON, 1778

"While we are zealously performing the duties of good Citizens and Soldiers, we certainly ought not to be inattentive to the higher duties of Religion. To the distinguished Character of Patriot, it should be our highest Glory to add the more distinguished Character of Christian. The signal Instances of providential Goodness which we have experienced . . . demand from us in a peculiar manner the warmest returns of Gratitude and Piety to the Supreme Author of all Good."

"No people can be bound to acknowledge and adore the invisible hand which conducts the affairs of men more than the people of the United States. Every step by which they have advanced to the character of an independent nation seems to have been distinguished by some token of providential agency."

"It is the duty of all nations to acknowledge the providence of Almighty God, to obey His will, to be grateful for His benefits and humbly to implore His protection and favor."

WASHINGTON'S LETTER TO THE GOVERNORS OF THE 13 STATES

"I now make it my earnest prayer that God would have you and the states over which you preside, in His holy protection . . . and finally, that He would most graciously be pleased to dispose us all to do justice, to love mercy, and to demean ourselves with that charity, humility, and pacific temper of mind which were the characteristics of the Divine Author of our blessed religion."

LETTER BY WASHINGTON TO THE PRESIDENT OF CONGRESS

"On November 15, 1781, after the surrender at Yorktown, Washington wrote to the president of Congress: *'I take particular pleasure in acknowledging that the interposing hand of Heaven . . . has been most conspicuous and remarkable.'* He declared the day after the surrender to be a day of thanksgiving, and his troops were directed to attend religious services."[1]

BENJAMIN FRANKLIN'S FAITH IN ONE GOD

Writing to Ezra Stiles, president of Yale University, Franklin answered Stiles' question in these words:

"You desire to know something of my religion . . . Here is my creed. I believe in one God, Creator of the Universe. That he governs by his Providence. That he ought to be worshipped. That the most acceptable service we render to him is doing

---

1. Mac and Tate, *Under God*, 37.

good to his other children. That the soul of man is immortal, and will be treated with justice in another life respecting his conduct in this.

"I shall only add, respecting myself, that having experienced the good of that Being in conducting me prosperously through a long life, I have no doubt of its continuance in the next, though without the smallest conceit of meriting such goodness."

Chapter 4

The Declaration of Independence

Our Declaration of Independence, signed by fifty-six delegates of the thirteen colonies, was both visionary and courageous, cutting the ties of the colonies to the English crown. Thus, its framers were considered by the British Crown to be treasonous and subject to death. Thomas Jefferson apparently created the draft of the declaration, with Benjamin Franklin and others editing it. It came out of such documents as Britain's *Magna Charta* and colonial charters.

As with former documents, the Declaration of Independence acknowledged the dependence of the colonists on Divine Providence. Here is the document in part:

"When in the Course of human events, it becomes necessary for one people to dissolve the political bands which have connected them with another, and to assume among the powers of the earth, the separate and equal station to which the Laws of Nature and of Nature's God entitle them, a decent respect to the opinions of mankind requires that they should declare the causes which impel them to the separation.

"We hold these truths to be self-evident, that all men are created equal, that they are endowed by their Creator with certain unalienable Rights, that among these are Life, Liberty

and the pursuit of Happiness. That to secure these rights, Governments are instituted among Men, deriving their just powers from the consent of the governed, That whenever any Form of Government becomes destructive to the these ends, it is the Right of the People to alter or to abolish it, and to institute new Government, laying its foundation on such principles and organizing its powers in such form, as to them shall seem most likely to effect their Safety and Happiness. Prudence, indeed, will dictate that Governments long established should not be changed for light and transient causes; and accordingly all experience hath shewn, that mankind are more disposed to suffer, while evils are sufferable, than to right themselves by abolishing the forms to which they are accustomed. But when a long train of abuses and usurpations, pursuing invariably the same Object evinces a design to reduce them under absolute Despotism, it is their right, it is their duty, to throw off such Government, and to provide new Guards for their future security . . .

"We, therefore, the Representatives of the united States of America, in General Congress, Assembled, appealing to the Supreme Judge of the world for the rectitude of our intentions, do, in the Name, and by Authority of the good People of these Colonies, solemnly publish and declare, That these united Colonies are, and of Right ought to be Free and Independent States, that they are Absolved from all Allegiance to the British Crown, and that all political connection between them and the State of Great Britain, is and ought to be totally dissolved; and that as Free and Independent States, they have full Power to levy War, conclude Peace, contract Alliances, establish Commerce, and to do all other Acts and Things which Independent States may of right do. —And for the support

of this Declaration, with a firm reliance on the protection of Divine Providence, we mutually pledge to each other our Lives, our Fortunes, and our sacred Honor."

IS GOD IN THIS DOCUMENT?

What references to God appear in the Declaration of Independence?

- Endowed by their creator with certain unalienable rights.
- Appeal to the Supreme Judge of the world.
- A firm reliance on the protection of Divine Providence.

Isn't that clear enough? Did not the framers understand and appeal to Divine blessings on their efforts?

WHAT HAPPENED TO THE SIGNERS?

Fifty-six men signed the Declaration of Independence. Twenty-four were lawyers and jurists. Eleven were merchants. Nine were farmers and large landholders. All were educated men of financial means. What happened to them for having signed that document?

Five were captured by the British as traitors and were tortured before dying. Twelve had their homes destroyed. Two lost their sons in the Revolutionary War. Another had his two sons captured. Nine died from wounds or deprivations suffered during the war. One saw his fleet of ships destroyed by the British Navy. One lost his family and possessions. Another lost his home and possessions, and saw his wife imprisoned. Another was driven from his home and his dying wife. Their thirteen children fled for their lives. So thirty of the fifty-six paid a high price indeed for their stand for liberty under God.

By 1832, fifty-six years later, all the signers of the Declaration had passed on except one lone survivor, Charles Carroll, who died that year at age ninety-five. Six years before, on the fiftieth Anniversary of the Declaration of Independence, Carroll penned some more of those lines that are epical.

He was thankful to almighty God who had blessed him through the Lord Jesus Christ to have lived to be eighty-nine and to have had a part in the emancipation of his country. He signed the Declaration on August 2, 1776, recommending to future generations the principles of that document. He prayed that *"the civil and religious liberties that they have secured for my country may be perpetuated to the remotest posterity and extend to the whole family of man."*

SAMUEL ADAMS ON RESTORING GOD AS SOVEREIGN IN OUR NATION

Upon signing the Declaration of Independence, Adams said, *"We have this day restored the Sovereign, to whom alone men ought to be obedient. He reigns in heaven and . . . from the rising to the setting sun, may His Kingdom come."*[1]

---

1. Mac and Tate, *Under God*, 19.

PROCLAMATION BY THE COMMONWEALTH OF MASSACHUSETTS, JANUARY 23, 1776

"It is a maxim that in every government there must exist, somewhere, a supreme, sovereign, absolute, and uncontrollable power; but this power resides always in the body of the people, and it never was, or can be, delegated to one man, or a few; the great Creator has never given to men a right to vest others with authority over them, unlimited either in duration or degree."

Chapter 5

Articles of Confederation and the Constitution

IN ADDITION to the Declaration of Independence, two other important documents shaped the fledgling United States into a union of states. These were the Articles of Confederation and the U.S. Constitution.

THE ARTICLES OF CONFEDERATION

Following is the conclusion of the Articles of Confederation, which was ratified in 1781 and preceded our Federal Constitution:

"And Whereas it hath pleased the Great Governor of the World to incline the hearts of the legislatures we respectively represent in Congress, to approve of, and to authorize us to ratify the said Articles of Confederation and perpetual Union. Know Ye that we the undersigned delegates, by virtue of the power and authority to us given for that purpose, do by these presents, in the name and in behalf of our respective constituents, fully and entirely ratify and confirm each and every of the said Articles of Confederation and perpetual Union, and all and singular the matters and things therein contained: And we do further solemnly plight and engage

the faith of our respective constituents, that they shall abide by the determinations of the United States in Congress assembled, on all questions, which by the said Confederation are submitted to them. And that the Articles thereof shall be inviolably observed by the States we respectively represent, and that the Union shall be perpetual."

The Articles of Confederation displayed a dependence upon God for the success of this infant nation: *"Whereas it hath pleased the Great Governor of the World to incline the hearts of the legislatures we respectively represent in Congress..."*

THE CONSTITUTION

Fifty-two of the fifty-five founders of the Constitution were members of established orthodox churches in the colonies.

However, the Constitution, adopted September 17, 1787, makes no direct reference to God or religion, except for stating that one's religious faith may not be a consideration in his or her election to public office. However, the First Amendment does refer to religion in these words:

"Congress shall make no law respecting an establishment of religion, or prohibiting the free exercise thereof..."

That wording has been the subject of much debate and many judicial decisions. It was meant to protect the citizens from ever having an official religion, such as they had experienced back in England. It forever prohibited Congress from establishing a state religion, or prohibiting the free exercise of religion by the citizens.

Over the years this statement has been turned upside-down. Now it means that there must be an absolute separation, at all levels, between church and state. In practical terms, it has been construed to prohibit any encroachment on the government by religion. The *"free exercise of religion"* is no longer being protected. On the contrary, in various realms of activity, religion is limited in its expression . . . all on the grounds that such expression is "unconstitutional." Yet, as we shall see later, documents, inscriptions and monuments even in our federal buildings and grounds portray frequent references to Bible characters and passages.

CONCLUSION

Do you see something highly inconsistent in all of this? Why is it legal for references to God and the Bible to be permitted at the highest level, even in oaths of office, and illegal for lower levels of government to use them?

Will the day ever come when the Supreme Court returns to the original wording and intent of Amendment 1? Or, will it, or lower courts, continue to hinder the free exercise of religion?

Chapter 6

Constitutions of the Fifty States

Has the thread of faith in Divine Providence permeated the state constitutions? In other words, once past the Declaration of Independence and the formation of the states, one by one, does faith in God enter into their constitutions?

Let us take a look the preambles for all fifty states:

Alabama (1901)—"Invoking the favor and guidance of *Almighty God,* we do ordain and establish the following constitution."

Alaska (1956)—"We, the people of Alaska, *grateful to God* and to those who founded our nation and pioneered this great land..."

Arizona (1911)—"We, the people of the State of Arizona, grateful to *Almighty God* for our liberties, do ordain this Constitution."

Arkansas (1874)—grateful to Almighty God for the privilege of choosing our own form of government..."

California (1879)—"We the people of the State of California, grateful to *Almighty God* for our freedom..."

Colorado (1876)—"We, the people of Colorado, with profound reverence for the *Supreme Ruler of the Universe*..."

Constitutions of the Fifty States 31

- **Connecticut (1818)**—"The people of Connecticut, acknowledging with gratitude the good *Providence of God*..."
- **Delaware (1897)**—"Through *Divine Goodness* all men have, by nature, the rights of worshipping and serving their *Creator*..."
- **Florida (1885)**—"We, the people of the State of Florida, grateful to *Almighty God* for our constitutional liberty, establish this Constitution..."
- **Georgia (1777)**—"We the people of Georgia, relying upon protection and guidance of *Almighty God,* do ordain and establish this Constitution."
- **Hawaii (1959)**—We the people of Hawaii, grateful for *Divine Guidance,* establish this Constitution."
- **Idaho (1889)**—"We the people of the State of Idaho, grateful to *Almighty God* for our freedom..."
- **Illinois (1870)**—"We the people of the State of Illinois, grateful to *Almighty God* for the civil, political and religious liberty which He hath so long permitted us to enjoy and looking to *Him* for a blessing on our endeavors..."
- **Indiana (1851)**—We the people of the State of Indiana, grateful to *Almighty God* for the free exercise of the right to choose our form of government..."
- **Iowa (1857)**—"We, the people of the State of Iowa, grateful to the *Supreme Being* for the blessing hitherto enjoyed, and feeling on dependence on *Him* for the continuation of these blessings..."
- **Kansas (1859)**—"We, the people of Kansas, grateful to *Almighty God* for the civil and religious privileges establish this Constitution.

Kentucky (1891)—"We, the people of the Commonwealth are grateful to *Almighty God* for the civil, political religious liberties..."

Louisiana (1921)—"We, the people of the State of Louisiana, grateful to *Almighty God* for civil, political and religious liberties we enjoy..."

Maine (1820)—"We, the people of Maine, acknowledging with grateful hearts the goodness of the *Sovereign Ruler of the Universe* ... and imploring His aid and direction..."

Maryland (1776)—We, the people of the State of Maryland, grateful to *Almighty God* for our civil and religious liberty..."

Massachusetts (1780)—"We, the people of Massachusetts, acknowledging with grateful hearts, the goodness of the Great Liberator of the Universe ... In the course of His Providence..."

Michigan (1908)—"We, the people of the State of Michigan, grateful to *Almighty God* for the blessings of freedom establish this Constitution..."

Minnesota (1857)—"We, the people of the State of Minnesota, grateful to *God* for our civil and religious liberty..."

Mississippi (1890)—"We, the people of Mississippi, in convention assembled, grateful to *Almighty God*, and invoking *His* blessing in our work..."

Missouri (1845)—"We, the people of Missouri, with profound reverence for the *Supreme Ruler of the Universe*, and grateful for *His* good, establish this Constitution."

Montana (1889)—"We, the people of Montana, grateful to *Almighty God* for the blessing of liberty establish this Constitution."

Nebraska (1875)—"We, the people, grateful to *Almighty God* for our freedom, establish this Constitution."

New Hampshire (1792)—"Every individual has a natural and unalienable right to worship *God* according to the dictates of his own conscience..."

New Jersey (1947)—"We, the people of the State of New Jersey, grateful to *Almighty God* for the civil and religious liberty which He hath so long permitted us to enjoy, and looking to Him for a blessing upon our endeavors to secure and transmit the same unimpaired to succeeding generations, do ordain and establish this Constitution."

New Mexico (1911)—"We, the people of New Mexico, grateful to *Almighty God* for the blessings of liberty..."

New York (1846)—"We, the people of the State of New York, grateful to *Almighty God* for our freedom, in order to secure its blessings..."

North Carolina (1868)—"We, the people of the State of North Carolina, grateful to *Almighty God* the Sovereign Ruler of Nations, for our civil, political and religious liberties and acknowledging our dependence upon *Him* for the continuance of those..."

North Dakota (1889)—"We, the people of North Dakota, grateful to *Almighty God* for the blessings of civil and religious liberty, do ordain..."

Ohio (1852)—"We, the people of the State of Ohio, grateful to *Almighty God* for our freedom, to secure its blessings and to promote our common..."

Oklahoma (1907)—"Invoking the guidance of *Almighty God*, in order to secure and perpetuate the blessings of liberty... establish this..."

Oregon (1857)—"All men shall be secure in the Natural right, to worship *Almighty God* according to the dictates of their consciences..."

Pennsylvania (1776)—"We, the people of Pennsylvania, grateful to *Almighty God* for the blessings of civil and religious liberty, and humbly invoking *His* guidanc..."

Rhode Island (1842)—"We, the people of the State of Rhode Island, grateful to *Almighty God* for the civil and religious liberty which He has so long permitted us to enjoy, and looking to Him for blessing..."

South Carolina (1778)—"We, the people of the State of South Carolina, grateful to *God* for our liberties, do ordain and establish this Constitution."

South Dakota (1796)—"We, the people of South Dakota, grateful to *God* for our civil and religious liberties..."

Tennessee (1845)—"That all men have a natural and indefeasible right to worship *Almighty God* according to the dictates of their conscience..."

Texas (1845)—We, the people of the Republic of Texas, acknowledging with gratitude the grace and beneficence of *God*..."

Utah (1896)—"Grateful to *Almighty God* for life and liberty, we establish this Constitution..."

Vermont (1777)—"Whereas all government ought to enable the individuals who compose it to enjoy their natural rights which the *Author and Existence* has bestowed on man..."

Virginia (1776)—"Religion, or the duty which we owe our *Creator*, can be directed only by Reason and that is the mutual duty of all to practice Christian Forbearance, Love and Charity towards each other..."

Washington (1889)—"We, the people of the State of Washington, grateful to the *Supreme Ruler of the Universe* for our liberties, do ordain this Constitution.

West Virginia (1872)—"Since through *Divine Providence* we enjoy the blessings of civil, political and religious liberty, we, the people of West Virginia reaffirm our faith in and constant reliance upon *God*..."

Wisconsin (1848)—"We, the people of Wisconsin, grateful to *God* for our freedom, domestic tranquility..."

Wyoming (1890)—"We, the people of the State of Wyoming, grateful to *God* for our civil, political, and religious liberties establish this constitution..."

CONCLUSION

Did you note that every one of the fifty states mentioned God in one wording or another, acknowledging his providence and their reliance on him. "But," you may say, "this may have been true of a more unsophisticated mindset among the framers of the earlier states' constitutions."

Oh? Then what about Alaska and Hawaii? Did their constitutions, written in 1956 and 1959, respectively, contain references to God and reliance on Him? Yes, they did. That must mean that all fifty states recognized, when their constitutions were framed, that God is almighty and supreme over the affairs of nations. Every state and all of is inhabitants are under the control of the God who creates and abolishes governments and their leaders as he wills. The writers and signers of our state constitutions recognized these facts.

Chapter 7

Other Post-Revolution Documents

GOD DIDN'T die in our nation following its launching. During the period from the end of the Revolutionary War until the Civil War, federal leaders continued to invoke God. Following are just a few of their statements:

BENJAMIN FRANKLIN, DELEGATE TO THE CONSTITUTIONAL CONVENTION OF 1787

"I therefore beg leave to move that henceforth prayers imploring the assistance of Heaven and its blessings on our deliberations be held in this Assembly every morning before we proceed to business."

This proposal was adopted in 1789. Salaried chaplains were appointed for each house of Congress. This practice still continues, with prayer offered before each daily meeting of Congress. Note: This is amazing, considering the supposed wall of separation between church and state.

"When the government moved to Washington, DC, Christian worship took place, not only in the House, but also in the Supreme Court [and the] War And Treasury Buildings."[1]

---

1. Church 2007:5.

Franklin also had this to say about God's governing nations:

"I've lived, sir, a long time, and the longer I live, the more convincing proofs I see that God governs in the affairs of men. If a sparrow cannot fall to the ground without His notice, is it probable that an empire can rise without His aid? We've been assured in the sacred writings that unless the Lord builds the house, they labor in vain that build it. I firmly believe this, and I also believe that with His concurring aid, we shall succeed in this political building no better than the builders of Babel."

JEDEDIAH MORSE, "THE FATHER OF AMERICAN GEOGRAPHY," ON GOD

"To the kindly influence of Christianity we owe that degree of civil freedom, and political and social happiness which mankind now enjoys... Whenever the pillars of Christianity shall be overthrown, our present republican forms of government—and all blessings which flow from them—must fall with them."

NOAH WEBSTER ON CHRISTIANITY AND GOVERNMENT

"No truth is more evident to any mind than that the Christian religion must be the basis of any government intended to secure the rights and privileges of a free people."

BENJAMIN RUSH AND RELIGION AND MORALS

"The only foundation for a useful education in a republic is to be laid in religion. Without this there can be no virtue, and without virtue there can be no liberty, and liberty is the object and life of all republican governments. Without religion, I believe that learning does much mischief to the morals and principles of mankind."

GEORGE WASHINGTON AND CHAPLAINS IN THE MILITARY

"During the War Washington lobbied Congress to maintain at least one clergyman for every two regiments and to increase their wages."[2]

WASHINGTON'S LETTERS TO CHURCHES

"From his letters to religious bodies, we can tease out three interlocking . . . imperatives:

- A national commitment to defend individual freedom of conscience
- Absolute government neutrality with respect to religion
- The obligation of religious bodies to uphold the law by supporting the constitutional powers invested in the government and its representatives.[3]

---

2. Ibid., 59.
3. Ibid., 67.

WASHINGTON'S STATEMENTS ON GOD'S PROVIDENCE

"It is the duty of all nations to acknowledge the providence of Almighty God, to obey his will, to be grateful for his benefits, and humbly to implore His protection and favor."

"O most Glorious God, in Jesus Christ my most merciful and loving Father, I acknowledge and confess my guilt, in the weak and imperfect performance of the duties of this day."[4]

WASHINGTON ON MORALITY AND RELIGION

"And let us with caution indulge the supposition that morality can be maintained without religion ... Reason and experience both forbid us to expect that national morality can prevail in exclusion of religious principles."

WASHINGTON'S INAUGURAL AND FAREWELL ADDRESSES

First Inaugural Address, April 30, 1789

From his first inaugural address, Washington acknowledged the impact of God on the founding of this new nation:

"No people can be bound to acknowledge and adore the invisible hand which conducts the affairs of men more than the people of the United States. Every step, by which they have advanced to the character of an independent nation, seems to have been distinguished by some token of providential agency."

---

4. From *Daily Sacrifice*, his personal prayer book.

Following are the concluding remarks from his First Inaugural Address:

"Having thus imported to you my sentiments, as they have been awakened by the occasion which brings us together, I shall take my present leave; but not without resorting once more to the benign parent of the human race, in humble supplication that since he has been pleased to favour the American people, with opportunities for deliberating in perfect tranquility, and dispositions for deciding with unparalleled unanimity on a form of Government, for the security of their Union, and the advancement of their happiness; so his divine blessing may be equally conspicuous *in the enlarged views, the temperate consultations, and the wise measures on which the success of this Government must depend."*

Declaration of a Day of Thanksgiving, November 1, 1777

"Forasmuch as it is the indispensable duty of all men to adore the superintending providence of Almighty God; to acknowledge with gratitude their obligation to him for benefits received, and to implore such farther blessings as they stand in need of; and it having pleased him in his abundant mercy not only to continue to us the innumerable bounties of his common providence, but also smile upon us in the prosecution of a just and necessary war, for the defense and establishment of our unalienable rights and liberties; particularly in that he hath been pleased in so great a measure to prosper the means used for the support of our troops and to crown our arms with most signal success:

"It is therefore recommended to the legislative or executive powers of these United States, to set apart Thursday, the 18th day of December next, for solemn thanksgiving and praise; that with one heart and one voice the good people may express the grateful feelings of their hearts, and consecrate themselves to the service of their divine benefactor; and that together with their sincere acknowledgments and offerings, they may join the penitent confession of their manifold sins, whereby they had forfeited every favor, and their humble and earnest supplication that it may please God, through the merits of Jesus Christ, mercifully to forgive and blot them out of remembrance; that it may please him graciously to afford his blessings on the governments of these states respectively, and prosper the public council of the whole; to inspire our commanders both by land and sea, and all under them, with that wisdom and fortitude which may render them fit instruments, under the providence of Almighty God, to secure for these United States the greatest of all blessings, independence and peace; that it may please him to prosper the trade and manufactures of the people and the labor of the husbandman, that our land may yield its increase; to take schools and seminaries of education, so necessary for cultivating the principles of true liberty, virtue and piety, under his nurturing hand, and to prosper the means of religion for the promotion and enlargement of that kingdom which consisteth in righteousness, peace and joy in the Holy Ghost.

"And it is further recommended, that servile labor, and such recreation as, though at other times innocent, may be unbecoming the purpose of this appointment, be omitted on so solemn an occasion."

Washington's Farewell Address, 1796

These are excerpts from his Farewell Address:

"*Of all the dispositions and habits which lead to political prosperity, religion and morality are indispensable supports. In vain would that man claim the tribute of patriotism, who should labor to subvert these great pillars of human happiness, these firmest props of the duties of men and citizens. The mere politician, equally with the pious man, ought to respect and to cherish them. A volume could not trace all their connections with private and public felicity. Let it simply be asked: Where is the security for property, for reputation, for life, if the sense of religious obligation desert the oaths which are the instruments of investigation in courts of justice? And let us with caution indulge the supposition that morality can be maintained without religion. Whatever may be conceded to the influence of refined education on minds of peculiar structure, reason and experience both forbid us to expect that national morality can prevail in exclusion of religious principle.*

"*It is substantially true that virtue or morality is a necessary spring of popular government. The rule, indeed, extends with more or less force to every species of free government. Who that is a sincere friend to it can look with indifference upon attempts to shake the foundation of the fabric? . . .*

"*Observe good faith and justice towards all nations; cultivate peace and harmony with all. Religion and morality enjoin this conduct; and can it be, that good policy does not equally enjoin it - It will be worthy of a free, enlightened, and at no distant period, a great nation, to give to mankind the magnanimous and too novel example of a people always guided by an exalted justice and benevolence. Who can doubt that, in the course of time and things, the fruits of such a plan would richly repay any temporary advantages which might be lost by a steady adherence to it ? Can it be that Providence has not connected the permanent felicity of a nation with its virtue? The experiment, at least, is recommended by every sentiment which ennobles human nature. Alas! is it rendered impossible by its vices . . .*

"Though, in reviewing the incidents of my administration, I am unconscious of intentional error, I am nevertheless too sensible of my defects not to think it probable that I may have committed many errors. Whatever they may be, I fervently beseech the Almighty to avert or mitigate the evils to which they may tend. I shall also carry with me the hope that my country will never cease to view them with indulgence; and that, after forty five years of my life dedicated to its service with an upright zeal, the faults of incompetent abilities will be consigned to oblivion, as myself must soon be to the mansions of rest."

In these addresses we see Washington's acknowledgement of the Supreme Authority over the affairs of the infant U.S.:

- *"Resorting once more to the benign parent of the human race . . ."*

- *"Though, in reviewing the incidents of my administration, I am unconscious of intentional error, I am nevertheless too sensible of my defects not to think it probable that I may have committed many errors. Whatever they may be, I fervently beseech the Almighty to avert or mitigate the evils to* which they may tend."

CHARLES CARROLL, SIGNER OF THE DECLARATION OF INDEPENDENCE

"Without morals a republic cannot subsist any length of time. They therefore who are decrying the Christian religion, whose morality is so sublime and pure . . . are undermining the solid foundation of morals, the best security for the duration of free governments."[5]

JOHN ADAMS

"Statesmen may plan and speculate for liberty, but it is religion and morality alone, which can establish the principles upon which freedom can securely stand."

"The general principles upon which the Fathers achieved independence were the general principles of Christianity . . . I will avow that I believed and now believe that these general principles of Christianity are as eternal and immutable as the existence and attributes of God."

"[The Fourth of July] ought to be commemorated as the day of deliverance by solemn acts of devotion to God almighty."[6]

JOHN ADAMS'S INAUGURAL ADDRESS,

---

5. Correspondence to James McHenry, Nov. 4, 1800.
6. In a letter to his wife Abigail on the day when the Declaration was signed.

MARCH 4, 1787

Following are paragraphs from his Inauguration speech:

"*I feel it to be my duty to add, if a veneration for the religion of a people who profess and call themselves Christians, and a fixed resolution to consider a decent respect for Christianity among the best recommendations for the public service, can enable me in any degree to comply with your wishes, it shall be my strenuous endeavor that this sagacious injunction of the two Houses shall not be without effect.*

"*With this great example before me, with the sense and spirit, the faith and honor, the duty and interest, of the same American people pledged to support the Constitution of the United States, I entertain no doubt of its continuance in all its energy, and my mind is prepared without hesitation to lay myself under the most solemn obligations to support it to the utmost of my power.*

"*And may that Being who is supreme over all, the Patron of Order, the Fountain of Justice, and the Protector in all ages of the world of virtuous liberty, continue His blessing upon this nation and its Government and give it all possible success and duration consistent with the ends of His providence.*"

Adams, too, confessed his reliance on God, as he assumed the presidency:

"*I feel it to be my duty to add, if a veneration for the religion of a people who profess and call themselves Christians, and a fixed resolution to consider a decent respect for Christianity among the best recommendations for the public service, can enable me in any degree to comply with your wishes . . .*"

"And may that Being who is supreme over all, the Patron of Order, the Fountain of Justice, and the Protector in all ages of the world of virtuous liberty, continue His blessing upon this nation and its Government and give it all possible success and duration consistent with the ends of His providence."

A decent respect for Christianity among the best recommendations for public service? Those words sound foreign to present-day requirements for public service.

JOHN ADAMS'S PROCLAMATION OF A NATIONAL DAY OF PRAYER

"As the safety and prosperity of nations ultimately and essentially depend on the protection and blessing of Almighty God; and the national acknowledgment of this truth is not only an indispensable duty which the people owe to Him, but a duty whose natural influence is favorable to the promotion of that morality and piety, without which social happiness cannot exist, nor the blessings of a free government be enjoyed; and as this duty, at all times incumbent, is so especially in seasons of difficulty and of danger, when existing or threatening calamities, the just judgments of God against prevalent iniquity are a loud call to repentance and reformation; and as the United States of America are at present placed in a hazardous and afflictive situation, by the unfriendly disposition, conduct and demands of a foreign power, evinced by repeated refusals to receive our messengers of reconciliation and peace, by depredations on our commerce, and the infliction of injuries on very many of our fellow citizens, while engaged in their lawful business on the seas—Under these considerations it has appeared to me that the duty of imploring the mercy and benediction of Heaven on our country, demands at this time a special attention from its inhabitants.

I have therefore thought it fit to recommend, that Wednesday, the ninth day of May next be observed throughout the United States, as a day of Solemn Humiliation, Fasting and Prayer; That the citizens of these states, abstaining on that day from their customary worldly occupations, offer their devout addresses to the Father of Mercies, agreeably to those forms or methods which they have severally adopted as the most suitable and becoming: That all religious congregations do, with the deepest humility, acknowledge before God the manifold sins and transgressions with which we are justly chargeable as individuals and as a nation; beseeching him, at the same time, of his infinite Grace, through the Redeemer of the world, freely to remit all our offences, and to incline us, by his holy spirit, to that sincere repentance and reformation which may afford us reason to hope for his inestimable favor and heavenly benediction; That it be made the subject of particular and earnest supplication, that our country may be protected from all the dangers which threaten it; that our civil and religious privileges may be preserved inviolate, and perpetuated to the latest generations; that our public councils and magistrates may be especially enlightened and directed at this critical period; that the American people may be united in those bonds of amity and mutual confidence, and inspired with that vigor and fortitude by which they have in times past been so highly distinguished, and by which they have obtained such invaluable advantages: That the health of the inhabitants of our land may be preserved, and their agriculture, commerce, fisheries, arts and manufactures be blessed and prospered: That the principles of genuine piety and sound morality may influence the minds and govern the lives of every description of our citizens; and that the blessings of peace, freedom, and pure religion, may be speedily extended to all the nations of the earth.

"And finally I recommend, that on the said day; the duties of humiliation and prayer be accompanied by fervent Thanksgiving to the bestower of every good gift, not only for having hitherto protected and preserved the people of these United States in the independent enjoyment of their religious and civil freedom, but also for having prospered them in a wonderful progress of population, and for conferring on them many and great favours conducive to the happiness and prosperity of a nation.

"Given under my hand and seal of the United States of America, at Philadelphia, this twenty-third day of March, in the year of our Lord one thousand seven hundred and ninety-eight, and of the Independence of the said States the twenty-second."

JOHN ADAMS'S STATEMENT ABOUT MORALITY AND RELIGION

"We have no government armed with power capable of contending with human passions unbridled by morality and religion. Our Constitution was made only for a moral and religious people. It is wholly inadequate to the government of any other."

SAMUEL ADAMS, 1776

"Let each citizen remember at the moment he is offering his vote that he is . . . executing one of the most solemn trusts in human society for which he is accountable to God and his country."

"He who made all men hath made the truths necessary to human happiness obvious to all . . . Our forefathers opened the Bible to all."[7]

"Let divines and philosophers, statesmen and patriots, unite their efforts to renovate the age by impressing the minds of men with the importance of educating their little boys and girls, inculcating in the minds of youth the fear and love of the Deity . . . and leading them in the study and practice of the exalted Christian system."[8]

MATHIAS BURNET, CLERGYMAN, 1803

"To God and posterity you are accountable for [your rights and your rulers] . . . Let not your children have reason to curse you for giving up those rights and prostrating those institutions which your fathers delivered to you."

JOHN HANCOCK

"I conjure [urge] you, by all that is dear, by all that is honorable, by all that is sacred, not only that ye pray but that ye act."

---

7. Speech delivered at the State House in Philadelphia August 1, 1776.

8. October 4, 1790.

THOMAS JEFFERSON'S INAUGURAL ADDRESS, MARCH 4, 1801

This excerpt is from the closing paragraph of his address:

"Relying, then, on the patronage of your good will, I advance with obedience to the work, ready to retire from it whenever you become sensible how much better choice it is in your power to make. And may that Infinite Power which rules the destinies of the universe lead our councils to what is best, and give them a favorable issue for your peace and prosperity."

Jefferson, who had a generally different view of Christianity than most, still realized the Infinite Power who rules the destinies of the universe.

JEFFERSON'S "WALL OF SEPARATION" LETTER TO THE DANBURY BAPTISTS

"Believing with you that religion is a matter which lies solely between man his God, that he owes account to none other for his faith or his worship, that the legislative powers of government reach actions only, and not opinions, I contemplate with sovereign reverence that act of the whole American people which declared that their legislature should 'make no law respecting the establishment of religion, or prohibiting the free exercise thereof,' thus building a wall of separation between church and state."

" . . . Jefferson's letter . . . remains the single most influential presidential document in the history of American church-state relations . . . "[9]

---

9. Church, 165.

I must ask here why this private letter, which never passed through Congress for action, became the standard by which expressions by any religious group on anything related to government be construed as unconstitutional? Courts can impose their collective will on the public, but the public cannot impose spiritual influence on government, because of the "sacred" wall of separation between church and state. I am totally opposed to any official state religion, but also am totally opposed to the gagging by the courts of the free expression of religion.

JEFFERSON'S STATEMENT ON LIBERTIES AS THE GIFT OF GOD

"And can the liberties of a nation be thought secure when we have removed them from their only firm basis, a conviction in the minds of the people that these liberties are the gift of God? That they are not to be violated but with His wrath? Indeed I tremble for my country when I reflect that God is just and that His justice cannot sleep forever."

JAMES MADISON'S FIRST INAUGURAL ADDRESS, MARCH 4, 1809

This is taken from the last paragraph in his speech:

"But the source to which I look or the aids which alone can supply my deficiencies is in the well-tried intelligence and virtue of my fellow-citizens, and in the counsels of those representing them in the other departments associated in the care of the national interests. In these my confidence will under every difficulty be best placed, next to that which we have all

been encouraged to feel in the guardianship and guidance of that Almighty Being whose power regulates the destiny of nations, whose blessings have been so conspicuously dispensed to this rising Republic, and to whom we are bound to address our devout gratitude for the past, as well as our fervent supplications and best hopes for the future."

Margaret Smith, A participant in the Inauguration, wrote to her sister that Madison reaffirmed this principle: "To avoid the slightest interference with the rights of conscience or the functions of religion, so wisely exempted from civil jurisdiction . . ."

MADISON'S STATEMENT ON SUBJECTION TO GOD

"Before any man can be considered as a member of civil society, he must be considered as a subject of the Governor of the Universe."

MADISON ON THE TEN COMMANDMENTS

"We have staked the whole future of American civilization not on the power of government, far from it. We have staked the future . . . upon the capacity of each and all of us to govern ourselves, to control ourselves, to sustain ourselves according to the Ten Commandments of God."

JAMES MONROE'S FIRST INAUGURAL ADDRESS, MARCH 4, 1817

This is from his closing sentence:

"Relying on the aid to be derived from the other departments of the Government, I enter on the trust to which I have been called by the suffrages of my fellow-citizens with my fervent prayers to the Almighty that He will be graciously pleased to continue to us that protection which He has already so conspicuously displayed in our favor."

JOHN QUINCY ADAMS ON THE CORNERSTONE OF GOVERNMENT

"Is it not in the chain of human events, the birthday of the nation is indissolubly linked with the birthday of the Savior?—that it forms a leading event in the progress of the Gospel dispensation? Is it not that the Declaration of Independence first organized the social compact on the foundation of the Redeemer's mission upon earth?—That it laid the cornerstone of human government upon the first precepts of Christianity?"[10]

JOHN JAY'S FAITH IN CHRIST

John Jay, first Supreme Court Justice and president of the Continental Congress, wrote this in his Last Will and Testament, 1829:

"Unto Him who is the author and giver of all good, I render sincere and humble thanks for His manifold and unmerited blessings, and especially for our redemption and salvation by His Beloved Son."

---

10. 1837, in a Fourth of July speech at Newburyport, Massachusetts.

Other Post-Revolution Documents 55

GEORGE MASON'S STATEMENT OF FAITH

Mason was a participant in the formation of the Constitution and primary motivator for inclusion of a Bill of Rights. Here is what he said in his Last Will and Testament:

"My soul, I resign into the hands of my Almighty Creator . . . humbly hoping for His unbounded mercy, through the merits of my blessed Savior, a remission of my sins."

ANDREW JACKSON'S FIRST INAUGURAL ADDRESS, MARCH 4, 1829

"And a firm reliance on the goodness of that Power whose providence mercifully protected our national infancy, and has since upheld our liberties in various vicissitudes, encourages me to offer up my ardent supplications that He will continue to make our beloved country the object of His divine care and gracious benediction."

WILLIAM HENRY HARRISON'S FIRST INAUGURAL ADDRESS, MARCH 4, 1841

This excerpt is from the second-to-last paragraph of his almost two-hour-long speech:

"I deem the present occasion sufficiently important and solemn to justify me in expressing to my fellow-citizens a profound reverence for the Christian religion and a thorough conviction that sound morals, religious liberty, and a just sense of religious responsibility are essentially connected with all true and lasting happiness; and to that good Being who has blessed us by the gifts of civil and religious freedom, who watched over and prospered the labors of our fathers and has

hitherto preserved to us institutions far exceeding in excellence those of any other people, let us unite in fervently commending every interest of our beloved country in all future time."

JAMES K. POLK'S INAUGURAL ADDRESS, MARCH 4, 1845

This is from his closing paragraph:

"*Confidently relying upon the aid and assistance of the coordinate departments of the Government in conducting our public affairs, I enter upon the discharge of the high duties which have been assigned me by the people, again humbly supplicating that Divine Being who has watched over and protected our beloved country from its infancy to the present hour to continue His gracious benedictions upon us, that we may continue to be a prosperous and happy people.*"

ZACHARY TAYLOR'S INAUGURAL ADDRESS, MARCH 5, 1849

His speech ended with these words:

"*In conclusion I congratulate you, my fellow-citizens, upon the high state of prosperity to which the goodness of Divine Providence has conducted our common country. Let us invoke a continuance of the same protecting care which has led us from small beginnings to the eminence we this day occupy, and let us seek to deserve that continuance by prudence and moderation in our councils, by well-directed attempts to assuage the bitterness which too often marks unavoidable differences of opinion, by the promulgation and practice of just and liberal principles, and by an enlarged patriotism, which shall acknowledge no limits but those of our own widespread Republic."*

JAMES BUCHANAN'S INAUGURAL ADDRESS, MARCH 4, 1857

This is from his closing sentence:

"I shall now proceed to take the oath prescribed by the Constitution, whilst humbly invoking the blessing of Divine Providence on this great people."

Other inaugural addresses included similar words as these above. They can be verified by searching presidential inaugural addresses on the Internet. All of them together make for a very loud shout of faith in and dependence upon God.

FREEDOM OF RELIGION OR FREEDOM FROM RELIGION?

Our Founding Fathers wanted no part of a government sponsored or directed religion. They wanted the states and individuals to be free to practice their faith unhindered by federal control or law. However, they recognized the absolute need for faith, morals, and knowledge, if our fledgling nation was to prosper. In 1787 Congress passed the Northwest Ordinance, which dealt with settling lands north of the Ohio River. Article 3 of that ordinance opens with these words:

> *"Religion, morality and knowledge being necessary to good government and the happiness of mankind, schools and the means of education shall forever be encouraged."*

We see, then, public education involved the teaching of religious and moral values. It is a sad commentary on our times that such is not the case in most public schools. Yet, remember what Washington said in his farewell address about religion and morality:

> *"Of all the dispositions and habits which lead to political prosperity, religion and morality are indispensable supports ... and let us with caution indulge the supposition that morality can be maintained without religion ... Reason and experience both forbid us to expect that national morality can prevail to the exclusion of religious principle."*

Attorney Don Powers, who teaches courses on the U.S. Constitution, observes about this entire matter of freedom of religion vs. freedom from religion:

> *"The founders' message of no freedom without religion positions religion as an indispensable founding principle. The government encouraged religious practices through its actions in order to strengthen the moral fiber of the country, but the federal government, including its courts, could take no action relative to religion. This non-action is the real meaning of the separation of church and state."*[11]

Yet, as we have pointed out, the courts, in their politically-correct zeal, have legislated against freedom of religion. How? By their decisions against freedom of religious expression.

---

11. Powers, "No Freedom."

CONCLUSION

Can there be any doubt that, regardless of their individual interpretation of God's teachings, our Founding Fathers and early presidents all believed in Divine Providence and expressed this in their speeches and writings? Our responsibility today is not to separate religion from government and life in general, but to instill our generation and those that follow the basic elements of the Christian faith and morality that made our nation great in the first place.

Chapter 8

Lincoln's Addresses

It was Lincoln's burden to carry his nation through the gut-wrenching agony of the Civil War. Often, the outcome was very much in doubt. Often, it hung in the balance. An agonized Lincoln felt the serious need for divine guidance as he attempted to bring the war to a close and to heal the nation's wounds. Here are some of his remarks that reflect his faith in God as Captain of our nation's fate.

SECOND INAUGURAL ADDRESS

This is the conclusion of Lincoln's Second Inaugural Address, given March 4, 1865:

"*With malice toward none; with charity for all; with firmness in the right, as God gives us to see the right, let us strive on to finish the work we are in; to bind up the nation's wounds; to care for him who shall have borne the battle, and for his widow, and his orphan—to do all which may achieve and cherish a just, and lasting peace, among ourselves, and with all nations.*"

As we see in these words, Lincoln relied upon God to help him see the right.

"My great concern is not whether God is on our side. My great concern is to be on God's side."

DECLARATION OF A NATIONAL DAY OF PRAYER AND FASTING

"It is fit and becoming in all people, at all times, to acknowledge and revere the Supreme Government of God; to bow in humble submission to His chastisement; to confess and deplore their sins and transgressions in the full conviction that the fear of the Lord is the beginning of wisdom; and to pray, with all fervency and contrition, for the pardon of their past offenses, and for a blessing upon their present and prospective action."

GETTYSBURG ADDRESS, NOVEMBER 19, 1863

Gettysburg, the bloodiest battle ever on American soil and possibly the turning point of the Civil War, found thousands of war dead. Because of this, a federal cemetery was marked out at the site for these honored dead.

At the dedication of the Gettysburg National Cemetery, the famous orator, Edward Everett Hale, was asked by the organizing committee to give a major address. He did and it lasted for about two hours. Few remember now any of his speech. President Lincoln was asked "to give a few appropriate remarks," only as a courtesy to him as president. But what he said still echoes throughout our history. In his "few appropriate words" he spoke from his heart with memorable poetic phrases. Here is his address:

"Four score and seven years ago our fathers brought forth on this continent a new nation, conceived in Liberty, and dedicated to the proposition that all men are created equal.

"Now we are engaged in a great civil war, testing whether that

nation, or any nation, so conceived and so dedicated, can long endure. We are met on a great battle-field of that war. We have come to dedicate a portion of that field, as a final resting place for those who here gave their lives that that nation might live. It is altogether fitting and proper that we should do this."But, in a larger sense, we cannot dedicate . . . we cannot consecrate . . . we cannot hallow this ground. The brave men, living and dead, who struggled here, have consecrated it, far above our poor power to add or detract. The world will little note, nor long remember what we say here, but it can never forget what they did here. It is for us the living, rather, to be dedicated here to the unfinished work which they who fought here have thus far so nobly advanced. It is rather for us to be here dedicated to the great task remaining before us— that from these honored dead we take increased devotion to that cause for which they gave the last full measure of devotion—that we here highly resolve that these dead shall not have died in vain—that this nation, under God, shall have a new birth of freedom—and that government of the people, by the people, for the people, shall not perish from the earth."

CONCLUSION

Did Lincoln recognize that our nation was under God's dominion? Certainly. Read again the last three lines. "Under God" is the key phrase here. Lincoln longed for a new birth of freedom following the war, but knew that this would never happen without power from on high.

Chapter 9

More Recent Presidential Addresses that Refer to God

LINCOLN WAS certainly not the last of our presidents who invoked God in their public addresses. Here are some examples:

ULYSSES S. GRANT'S FIRST INAUGURAL ADDRESS, MARCH 4, 1869

"In conclusion I ask patient forbearance one toward another throughout the land, and a determined effort on the part of every citizen to do his share toward cementing a happy union; and I ask the prayers of the nation to Almighty God in behalf of this consummation."

JAMES A. GARFIELD'S FIRST INAUGURAL ADDRESS, MARCH 4, 1881

From his last paragraph:
"I shall greatly rely upon the wisdom and patriotism of Congress and of those who may share with me the responsibilities and duties of administration, and, above all, upon our efforts to promote the welfare of this great people and their

Government I reverently invoke the support and blessings of Almighty God."

GROVER CLEVELAND'S FIRST INAUGURAL ADDRESS, MARCH 4, 1885

From his last paragraph:

"And let us not trust to human effort alone, but humbly acknowledging the power and goodness of Almighty God, who presides over the destiny of nations, and who has at all times been revealed in our country's history, let us invoke His aid and His blessings upon our labors."

WILLIAM MCKINLEY'S FIRST INAUGURAL ADDRESS, MARCH 4, 1901

From his opening paragraph:

"In obedience to the will of the people, and in their presence, by the authority vested in me by this oath, I assume the arduous and responsible duties of President of the United States, relying upon the support of my countrymen and invoking the guidance of Almighty God. Our faith teaches that there is no safer reliance than upon the God of our fathers, who has so singularly favored the American people in every national trial, and who will not forsake us so long as we obey His commandments and walk humbly in His footsteps."

THEODORE ROOSEVELT'S INAUGURAL ADDRESS, MARCH 4, 1909

From his opening paragraph:

"My fellow-citizens, no people on earth have more cause to be thankful than ours, and this is said reverently, in no spirit of boastfulness in our own strength, but with gratitude to the Giver of Good who has blessed us with the conditions which have enabled us to achieve so large a measure of well-being and of happiness."

WOODROW WILSON'S FIRST INAUGURAL ADDRESS, MARCH 14, 1913

Following is the conclusion of his speech:

"And yet it will be no cool process of mere science. The Nation has been deeply stirred, stirred by a solemn passion, stirred by the knowledge of wrong, of ideals lost, of government too often debauched and made an instrument of evil. The feelings with which we face this new age of right and opportunity sweep across our heartstrings like some air out of God's own presence, where justice and mercy are reconciled and the judge and the brother are one. We know our task to be no mere task of politics but a task which shall search us through and through, whether we be able to understand our time and the need of our people, whether we be indeed their spokesmen and interpreters, whether we have the pure heart to comprehend and the rectified will to choose our high course of action. This is not a day of triumph; it is a day of dedication. Here muster, not the forces of party, but the forces of humanity. Men's hearts wait upon us; men's lives hang in the balance; men's hopes call upon us to say what we will do. Who shall live up to the great trust? Who dares fail to try? I summon all honest men, all patriotic, all forward-looking men, to my side. God helping me, I will not fail them, if they will but counsel and sustain me!"

Twice Wilson referred to God:

"The feelings with which we face this new age of right and opportunity sweep across our heartstrings like some air out of God's own presence, where justice and mercy are reconciled and the judge and the brother are one."

"I summon all honest men, all patriotic, all forward-looking men, to my side. God helping me, I will not fail them, if they will but counsel and sustain me!"

WARREN G. HARDING'S INAUGURAL ADDRESS, MARCH 14, 1921

These quotes are from his first and last two paragraphs:

"Standing in this presence, mindful of the solemnity of this occasion, feeling the emotions which no one may know until he senses the great weight of responsibility for himself, I must utter my belief in the divine inspiration of the founding fathers. Surely there must have been God's intent in the making of this new-world Republic.

"I accept my part with single-mindedness of purpose and humility of spirit, and implore the favor and guidance of God in His Heaven. With these I am unafraid, and confidently face the future.

"I have taken the solemn oath of office on that passage of Holy Writ wherein it is asked: "What doth the Lord require of thee but to do justly, and to love mercy, and to walk humbly with thy God?" This I plight to God and country."

HERBERT HOOVER'S INAUGURAL ADDRESS, MARCH 14, 1929

"This occasion is not alone the administration of the most sacred oath which can be assumed by an American citizen. It is a dedication and consecration under God to the highest office in service of our people. I assume this trust in the humility of knowledge that only through the guidance of Almighty Providence can I hope to discharge its ever-increasing burdens.

"I ask the help of Almighty God in this service to my country to which you have called me."

FRANKLIN D. ROOSEVELT'S FIRST INAUGURAL SPEECH, MARCH 4, 1933

"In this dedication of a Nation we humbly ask the blessing of God. May He protect each and every one of us. May He guide me in the days to come."

ROOSEVELT'S SECOND INAUGURAL SPEECH, JANUARY 20, 1937

"While this duty rests upon me I shall do my utmost to speak their purpose and to do their will, seeking Divine guidance to help us each and every one to give light to them that sit in darkness and to guide our feet into the way of peace."

ROOSEVELT'S THIRD INAUGURAL SPEECH, JANUARY 20, 1941

"We do not retreat. We are not content to stand still. As Americans, we go forward, in the service of our country, by the will of God."

Facing a severe depression, followed by the bloody Second World War, Roosevelt turned to God for support:

"We humbly ask the blessing of God. May He protect each and every one of us. May He guide me in the days to come."

". . . seeking Divine guidance to help us each and every one to give light to them that sit in darkness and to guide our feet into the way of peace."

". . . we go forward, in the service of our country, by the will of God."

DWIGHT D. EISENHOWER'S FIRST INAUGURAL SPEECH, JANUARY 20, 1953

This is Eisenhower's prayer at the opening of his speech:

"Almighty God, as we stand here at this moment my future associates in the executive branch of government join me in beseeching that Thou will make full and complete our dedication to the service of the people in this throng, and their fellow citizens everywhere. Give us, we pray, the power to discern clearly right from wrong, and allow all our words and actions to be governed thereby, and by the laws of this land. Especially we pray that our concern shall be for all the people regardless of station, race, or calling. May cooperation be permitted and be the mutual aim of those who, under the

concepts of our Constitution, hold to differing political faiths; so that all may work for the good of our beloved country and Thy glory. Amen."

JOHN F. KENNEDY'S INAUGURAL SPEECH, JANUARY 20, 1961

These are excerpts from his speech:

"My fellow citizens of the world: ask not what America will do for you, but what together we can do for the freedom of man.

"Finally, whether you are citizens of America or citizens of the world, ask of us the same high standards of strength and sacrifice which we ask of you. With a good conscience our only sure reward, with history the final judge of our deeds, let us go forth to lead the land we love, asking His blessing and His help, but knowing that here on earth God's work must truly be our own."

Kennedy too felt the serious need for God's blessing and help:

"... asking His blessing and His help, but knowing that here on earth God's work must truly be our own."

GERALD FORD'S INAUGURAL SPEECH, AUGUST 9, 1974

This is from his closing remarks:

"With all the strength and all the good sense I have gained from life, with all the confidence my family, my friends, and my dedicated staff impart to me, and with the good will of countless Americans I have encountered in recent *visits to forty States, I now solemnly reaffirm my promise I made to you last December 6: to uphold the Constitution, to do what is right as God gives me to see the right, and to do the very best I can for America."*

RONALD REAGAN'S INAUGURAL SPEECH, JANUARY 20, 1981

This is an excerpt from the middle of his address:

"Your dreams, your hopes, your goals are going to be the dreams, the hopes, and the goals of this administration, so help me God."

GEORGE H.W. BUSH'S FIRST INAUGURAL ADDRESS, JANUARY 20, 1989

This is the final line of his speech:

"Thank you. God bless you and God bless the United States of America."

BILL CLINTON'S FIRST INAUGURAL SPEECH, JANUARY 20, 1993

These words are from the opening and closing of his address:

"When our founders boldly declared America's independence to the world and our purposes to the Almighty, they knew that America, to endure, would have to change.

"And so, my fellow Americans, at the edge of the twenty-first century, let us begin with energy and hope, with faith and discipline, and let us work until our work is done. The scripture says, "And let us not be weary in well-doing, for in

due season, we shall reap, if we faint not." From this joyful mountaintop of celebration, we hear a call to service in the valley. We have heard the trumpets. We have changed the guard. And now, each in our way, and with God's help, we must answer the call. Thank you and God bless you all."

GEORGE W. BUSH'S FIRST INAUGURAL ADDRESS, JANUARY 20, 2001

"We are not this story's author, who fills time and eternity with his purpose. Yet his purpose is achieved in our duty, and our duty is fulfilled in service to one another. Never tiring, never yielding, never finishing, we renew that purpose today, to make our country more just and generous, to affirm the dignity of our lives and every life. This work continues. This story goes on. And an angel still rides in the whirlwind and directs this storm. God bless you all, and God bless America."

BARACK OBAMA'S INAUGURAL SPEECH, JANUARY 20, 2009

These are excerpts from his address:

"We remain a young nation, but in the words of Scripture, the time has come to set aside childish things. The time has come to reaffirm our enduring spirit; to choose our better history; to carry forward that precious gift, that noble idea, passed on from generation to generation: the God-given promise that all are equal, all are free, and all deserve a chance to pursue their full measure of happiness."

"This is the price and the promise of citizenship. This is the source of our confidence—the knowledge that God calls on us to shape an uncertain destiny."

"Thank you. God bless you. And God bless the United States of America."

CONCLUSION

These excerpts from presidential inaugurations all express reliance on God

as Sovereign over our nation. As recently as 2009 our newest president, Barak Obama, expressed his reliance on God and appealed to God for continued blessings on our nation. In all of this, where is separation of church and state? It is not there. All of our presidents, to one degree or another, have acknowledged the need for divine guidance.

Chapter 10

State of the Union Addresses and Reliance on God

From Washington onward presidents have given to Congress an annual "State of the Union" address. Excerpts from some of these follow:

GEORGE WASHINGTON'S INAUGURAL STATE OF THE UNION ADDRESS, 1790

Steven S. Goode observes on presidential State of the Union speeches:

"George Washington gave the first State of the Union message on Jan. 8, 1790, before a joint session of the House and Senate assembled in New York, then the nation's capital. The first president reminded Congress that America was a nation blessed by God in many ways and noted that 'a free people ought not only to be well armed, but well disciplined.'"[1]

---

1. Goode, 1996, page 22.

HARRY S. TRUMAN'S ADDRESS TO CONGRESS FOLLOWING THE DEATH OF FRANKLIN D. ROOSEVELT, APRIL 16, 1945

This excerpt is from his opening lines:

"It is with a heavy heart that I stand before you, my friends and colleagues, in the Congress of the United States.

"Only yesterday, we laid to rest the mortal remains of our beloved President, Franklin Delano Roosevelt. At a time like this, words are inadequate. The most eloquent tribute would be a reverent silence.

"Yet, in this decisive hour, when world events are moving so rapidly, our silence might be misunderstood and might give comfort to our enemies. In His infinite wisdom, Almighty God has seen fit to take from us a great man who loved, and was beloved by, all humanity."

And these words are from his closing lines:

"At this moment, I have in my heart a prayer. As I have assumed my heavy duties, I humbly pray Almighty God, in the words of King Solomon: 'Give therefore thy servant an understanding heart to judge thy people, that I may discern between good and bad; for who is able to judge this thy so great a people?' I ask only to be a good and faithful servant of my Lord and my people."

RONALD REAGAN'S STATE OF THE UNION ADDRESS. JANUARY 25, 1984

Here are his concluding words:

"Let us be sure that those who come after will say of us in our time, that in our time we did everything that could be

done. We finished the race; we kept them free; we kept the faith. Thank you very much. God bless you, and God bless America."

REAGAN ON ONE NATION UNDER GOD

"America needs God more than God needs America. If we ever forget that we are One Nation Under God, then we will be a nation gone under."

GEORGE W. BUSH'S STATE OF THE UNION ADDRESS, JANUARY. 2003

This is taken from the close of his speech, with comments by Gregory Dunn:

"In the final paragraph, Bush said, 'We do not claim to know all the ways of Providence, yet we can trust in them, placing our confidence in the loving God behind all of life and of history.' The implication is that any divine favor America possesses is the result not of its intrinsic merit but of God's gift. Such a gift may be taken from us; Scripture teaches that nations rise and fall by God's command. We do not know if any favor we have will be taken from us, though we do know what God requires of us. To be a nation 'under God' is to be, among other things, under his judgment—to be held accountable to his standards of justice. Liberty, for America, is not a divine birthright but a divine challenge. So we strive to be just.

"And we pray."

The most remarkable moment of Bush's speech is his closing: not 'God bless America,' as he often says, but the more *explicit 'May he guide us now, and may God continue to bless the United States of America.'*

This should not be missed: he closes with a prayer. As we strive to be just, we need guidance, so we humbly ask God for it. And we remember that the phrase 'God bless America' is not a statement or a command but a supplication. Liberty may be our right, but divine favor is not. So we humbly ask for it. Our situation is precarious. (It always is.) So we pray."[2]

GOD'S STATE OF THE UNION ADDRESS, 2011

This is imaginary, based on Scripture, but the words ring true for our day.

Jeremiah 14

"Then the Lord said unto me, The (politicians) prophesy lies in My name: I sent them not, neither have I commanded them, neither spake unto them: they prophesy unto you a false vision and divination, and a thing of nought, and the deceit of their heart."

Ezekiel 13

"And the word of the Lord came unto me, saying, Son of man, prophesy against the (politicians) of (America) that prophesy, and say thou unto them that prophesy out of their own hearts, Hear ye the word of the Lord; Thus saith the Lord God; 'Woe

---

2. Adapted from Dunn 2003: Ashbrook Center for Public Affairs, Ashland University, Ohio.

unto the foolish (politicians), that follow their own spirit, and have seen nothing!' O (America), thy prophets are like (a desert fox). They have seen vanity and lying divination, saying, The Lord saith: and the Lord hath not sent them: and they have made others to hope that they would confirm the word.

Have ye not seen a vain vision, and have ye not spoken a lying divination, whereas ye say, The Lord saith it; albeit I have not spoken? Therefore thus saith the Lord God; 'Because ye have spoken vanity, and seen lies, therefore, behold, I am against you,' saith the Lord God.

'And Mine hand shall be upon the (politicians) that see vanity, and that divine lies: they shall not be in the assembly of My people, neither shall they be written in the writing of the house of Israel, neither shall they enter into the land of Israel; and ye shall know that I am the Lord God.

Because, even because they have seduced My people, saying, Peace; and there was no peace; and one built up a wall, and, lo, others daubed it with untempered mortar: Say unto them which daub it with untempered mortar, that it shall fall: there shall be an overflowing shower; and ye, O great hailstones, shall fall; and a stormy wind shall rend it. Because with lies ye have made the heart of the righteous sad, whom I have not made sad; and strengthened the hands of the wicked, that he should not return from his wicked way, by promising him life: Therefore ye shall see no more vanity, nor divine divinations: for I will deliver My people out of your hand: and ye shall know that I am the Lord.'"

Ezekiel 22

"Her princes in the midst thereof are like wolves ravening the prey, to shed blood, and to destroy souls, to get dishonest gain. And her (politicians) have daubed them with untempered mortar, seeing vanity, and divining lies unto them, saying, Thus saith the Lord God, when the Lord hath not spoken. The people of the land have used oppression, and exercised robbery, and have vexed the poor and needy: yea, they have oppressed the stranger wrongfully. And I sought for a man among them, that should make up the hedge, and stand in the gap before Me for the land, that I should not destroy it: but I found none. Therefore (will) I (pour) out Mine indignation upon them; I (shall consume) them with the fire of My wrath: their own way (will) I (recompense) upon their heads, saith the Lord God."

It doesn't take that long to give the true state of the Union, does it?

CONCLUSION

Moral and spiritual references by American presidents are found throughout their state-of-the-union addresses.

Colleen J. Shogan writes this on the moral rhetoric used by American presidents:

"In the past several decades, presidents have highlighted the moral and religious dimensions of heir leadership . . . For example, in an obvious attempt to advertise his religiosity, Jimmy Carter took the oath of office in 1977 with not one, but two Bibles. All presidents now participate in the annual White House prayer breakfast. In his first act as president,

Ronald Reagan stated that future inaugurations should be declared a 'day of prayer.' When Richard Nixon resigned from office, his last words were a prayer: 'May God's grace be with you all in the days ahead.'"[3]

---

3. Shogan 2006:4.

Chapter 11

The View of Congress on Government and Religion

Today we have a greatly diminished view in government of the importance of the Christian faith as ruling in the decisions made by Congress. In fact, President Obama has stated to an international audience that our nation is not Christian, but rather, secular. Let us see what Congress said in the past on the Christian foundation of our government:

THE FAITH OF WASHINGTON AND ADAMS

The country's first two presidents, George Washington and John Adams, were firm believers in the importance of religion for republican government" (official congressional statement in the Library of Congress).

ESSENTIALITY OF FAITH IN GOVERNANCE

"Both the legislators and the public considered it appropriate for the national government to promote a non-denominational, non-polemical Christianity" (official congressional statement in the Library of Congress).

The View of Congress on Government and Religion

In 1782, Congress voted this resolution: *"The Congress of the United States recommends and approves the Holy Bible for use in all schools."*

Did you know this? Whatever happened to this resolution? Is it still in effect, or has it been cancelled? If so, when?

THANKSGIVING AND PRAYER

On September 25, 1789, upon approving of the Bill of Rights, Congress asked President Washington to declare a National Day of Thanksgiving and Prayer.

SENATE JUDICIARY COMMITTEE REPORT, JAN. 19, 1853

"We are a Christian people ... not because the law demands it, not to gain exclusive benefits or to avoid legal disabilities, but from choice and education; and in a land thus universally Christian, what is to be expected, what desired, but that we shall pay due regard to Christianity?"

HOUSE JUDICIARY COMMITTEE REPORT, MARCH 27, 1854

"At the time of the adoption of the Constitution and the amendments, the universal sentiment was that Christianity should be encouraged ... In this age there can be no substitute for Christianity ... That was the religion of the founders of the republic and they expected it to remain the religion of their descendants."

PRAYERS OPENING SESSIONS OF CONGRESS

Every session of Congress begins with a prayer by a preacher, whose salary has been paid by the taxpayer since 1777.

FOUNDING OF THE AMERICAN BIBLE SOCIETY (1776)

Shortly after creating the Declaration of Independence, Congress voted to found the American Bible Society and to purchase and import 20,000 copies of Scripture for the citizens of this new country.

CONCLUSION

Thomas Jefferson worried that the courts would overstep their authority and instead of interpreting the law, would begin making law an oligarchy—the rule of the few over the many. How, then, have we gotten to the point where everything we have done for more than 230 years in this country is now wrong and unconstitutional? As our president says, "Bad, bad America!

Chapter 12

The Supreme Court on Our Religious Heritage as a Nation

UNTIL 1948 the Supreme Court held to a conviction that government had no right to meddle in religious affairs, as long as religion did not overstep its bounds of functioning within the framework of American citizenship and loyalty to the principles upon which our nation was founded.

Then in 1948 came the first decision that became a precedent in jurisprudence. The court determined that religious instruction in public schools was a violation of the Establishment Clause in the First Amendment. "Establishment Clause" became the foundation from that point onward for all cases before the court that dealt with religion. Once that decision was reached, it became law; in fact, case law that determined all future decisions of that kind.

THE SUPREME COURT AND DECISIONS THAT AMOUNT TO LEGISLATION

So here we had the Supreme Court in effect enacting law, which was to be the prerogative solely of Congress. The Establishment Clause in the First Amendment became what it was never intended to be—a limit on the activities of churches. Congress was never to establish a state religion or to prohibit the free exercise of religion. So what happened? The Supreme Court stepped in and placed prohibitions on the free exercise of religion, something it had no right to do, all in the name of the Establishment Clause.

As a result, free expression of religion is more and more hindered, on the basis that it is somehow "unconstitutional." This monster has grown so large that charges are being made about many other areas, claiming that they too are unconstitutional. On the other hand, the Freedom of Speech Clause has been abused out of all proportion. In one city of my acquaintance nude dancing is permitted on the grounds that it represents "freedom of expression."

JOHN JAY, FIRST CHIEF-JUSTICE OF THE SUPREME COURT, ON THE BIBLE AND FAITH

"The Bible is the best of all books, for it is the word of God and teaches us the way to be happy in this world and the next. Continue there for to read it and to regulate your life by its precepts."

"Providence has give to our people the choice of their rulers, and it is the duty, as well as the privilege and interest of our Christian nation, to select and prefer Christians for their rulers."

JAMES WILSON, ORIGINAL JUSTICE OF THE SUPREME COURT

"Human law must rest its authority ultimately upon the authority of the law which is Divine . . . Far from being rivals

or enemies, religion and the law are twin sisters, friends, and mutual assistants. Indeed, these two sciences run into each other."

JOSEPH STORY, "FATHER OF AMERICAN JURISPRUDENCE," APPOINTED TO THE SUPREME COURT BY JAMES MADISON

"One of the beautiful boasts of our municipal jurisprudence is that Christianity is a part of the Common Law . . . There never has been a period in which the Common Law did not recognize Christianity as lying at its foundations . . . I verily believe Christianity necessary to the support of civil society."

Now let us turn to a court case from 1892 that defended Christianity, and then to the series of cases from 1948 onward that reversed the 1892 decision.

CHURCH OF THE HOLY TRINITY V UNITED STATES, FEBRUARY 20, 1892

"These and many other matters which might be noticed, add a volume of unofficial declarations to the mass of organic utterances that this is a Christian nation."

"Our lives and our institutions must necessarily be based upon and embody the teachings of the Redeemer of mankind. It is impossible that it should be otherwise; and in this sense and to this extent our civilization and our institutions are emphatically Christian."

MCCOLLUM V. BOARD OF EDUCATION DIST. 71, 333 U.S. 203 (1948)

The court found religions instruction in public schools a violation of the establishment clause and therefore unconstitutional. (*It should be noted here that Islam and other religions are taught in some public schools on the basis of their historical, social and cultural value—not Christianity, however.*)

BURSTYN V. WILSON, 72 S. CT. 777 (1952)

Government may not censor a motion picture because it is offensive to religious beliefs (*On what basis, Freedom of Expression?*).

TORCASO V. WATKINS. 367 U.S. 488 (1961)

Court held that the State of Maryland could not require applicants for public office to swear that they believed in the existence of God. The court unanimously held that a religious test violates the Establishment Clause. (*States cannot, but federal officials ask those sworn into office to say, "So help me God." Consistency, thy name is golden.*)

ENGEL V. VITALE, 82 S. CT. 1261 (1962)

Any kind of prayer, composed by public school districts, even non-denominational prayer, is unconstitutional government sponsorship of religion.

ABINGDON SCHOOL DISTRICT V. SCHEMPP, 347 U.S. 203 (1963)

Court found Bible reading over school intercoms unconstitutional.

MURRAY V. CURLETT, 374 U.S. 203 (1963)

Court found forcing a child to participate in Bible reading and prayer unconstitutional. (*This effectively denies children who want to participate the right to do so.*)

EPPERSON V. ARKANSAS, 89 S. CT. 266 (1968)

State statute banning teaching of evolution is unconstitutional. A state cannot alter any element in a course of study in order to promote a religious point of view. (*What the court does not admit is that evolution is a philosophical theory and not an empirical science as such. Freedom of enquiry should call for comparing the two philosophies, Christianity and Evolution.*)

LEMON V. KURTMAN, 91 S. CT. 2105 (1971)

The court established a three-part test for determining if an action of government violates the First Amendment's separation of church and state:

1. The government action must have a secular purpose.
2. The government's purpose must not be to inhibit or advance religion.

3. There must be no excessive entanglement between government and religion.

(*Yet, the government now inhibits religion in various ways.*)

STONE V. GRAHAM, 449 U.S. 39 1980

Court found posting of the Ten Commandments in schools unconstitutional. (*Yet, the Ten Commandments are on display in sculptures in the Supreme Court Building. Why there, but nowhere else?*)

WALLACE V. JAFFREE, 105 S. CT. 2573 (1985)

State's moment of silence at public school statute is unconstitutional where legislative record reveals that motivation for statute was the encouragement of prayer. Court majority was silent on whether "pure" moment of silence scheme, with no bias in favor of prayer or any other mental process, would be constitutional. (*Does this mean that if a student were to pray silently during a moment of silence, he or she would be violating the Constitution? And just what is a "pure" moment of silence? Is it the absence of all thought or reflection?*)

EDWARDS V. AQUILLARD, 107 S. CT. 2573 (1987)

Unconstitutional for state to require teaching of "creation science" in all instances in which evolution is taught. (*If the "science" of evolution is taught, why not give the students the opportunity to learn about another science? Academic enquiry demands an equal voice for divergent views on a subject, whether they are religious or secular.)*

ALLEGHENY COUNTY V. ACLU, 492 U.S. 573 (1989)

Court found that a nativity scene displayed inside a government building violates the Establishment Clause. (*Is such a scene really establishing a religion or merely acknowledging the existing predominant faith of our nation? Would a photo of the Sacred Mosque and the Kaa'ba in Mecca displayed in a government building be in violation of the Establishment Clause?*)

LEE V. WEISMAN, 112 S. CT. 2649 (1992)

It is unconstitutional for a school district to provide any clergy to perform nondenominational prayer at elementary or secondary school graduation. It involves government sponsorship of worship. Court majority was particularly concerned about psychological coercion to which children ... would be subjected, by having prayers that may violate their beliefs recited at their graduation ceremonies. (*And the probably considerable majority of students whose beliefs would not be prejudiced by such a practice? Have they no right to hear a prayer asking God's blessing on them? If they can hear no prayer, why then do Supreme Court Justices and Congress people hear official prayers?*)

CHURCH OF LUKUMI BABALU AVE., INC. V. HIEALEAH, 113 S. CT. 221

City's ban on killing animals for religious sacrifices, while allowing sport killing and hunting, was unconstitutional discrimination against the Santeria religion.

In a local experience, my city of Edmond, Oklahoma, was forced by the court to remove a cross as one symbol, along with those of an Indian motif, a covered wagon, a steam train and other elements of our city's history, from the city's seal. It was argued that the cross represented a religion and was therefore unconstitutional. The historical meaning of the cross was rejected. Strangely enough, it was a "Christian" religion that successfully had the cross removed.

ISTOOK AMENDMENT ON RELIGIOUS FREEDOM

The Istook Amendment was re-written and re-introduced into the House on May 8, 1997. The bill (H.J. Res 78) originally had 100 co-sponsors. This grew to 151 by March 1998-MAR. It reads:

"To secure the people's right to acknowledge God according to the dictates of conscience: The people's right to pray and to recognize their religious beliefs, heritage or traditions on public property, including schools, shall not be infringed. The government shall not require any person to join in prayer or other religious activity; initiate or designate school prayers, discriminate against religion, or deny equal access to a benefit on account of religion." (Note: This amendment failed.)

SUPREME COURT JUSTICE BLACKMUN'S STATEMENT ON CHURCH AND STATE

"When the government puts its imprimatur on a particular religion, it conveys a message of exclusion to all those who do not adhere to the favored beliefs. A government cannot be premised on the belief that all persons are created equal when it asserts that God prefers some."

HEIN V. FREEDOM FROM RELIGION FOUNDATION, 2007

By the usual five to four vote, a deeply divided court ruled that individual taxpayers and their organizations cannot sue the *Faith-Based and Community Initiatives* program of the federal government on the grounds that the latter violated the establishment clause of the First Amendment, unless Congress had specifically authorized the programs that supply the funding. Initiatives by the president and his administration that are paid out of general administration funding sources cannot be challenged.

JUSTICES'S VIEW ON CHURCH AND STATE

In Justice Renquist's reading of history, he believed that the establishment clause was intended only to prevent the establishment of a national church and to stop the federal government from demonstrating a preference for one religious body over others.

Justice Antonin Scalia made the following references to God and godly values, as reported by Wieseltier:[1] "Government draws its authority from God." "Our laws are derived from God." "The moral order is ordained by God." "Human affairs are directed by God." "God is the foundation of the state."

It is ironic that each session of the Supreme Court opens with the words, *"God save the United States and this honorable court."* Such statements cannot be made in lower courts, local government sessions or public schools. Yet, in the Supreme Court?

CONGRESS AND THE SUPREME COURT

Congress has not established a religion nor prohibited the free exercise of religion. It has merely sat by while justices and judges have continually whittled away at religious freedom. The list of decisions to limit religious expression is long and depressing. And it continues, today more than ever.

In 1947 there was a sudden and radical change of direction within the Supreme Court, which ignored every previous ruling of 160 years. The court ruled to affirm a wall of separation between Church and State in public classrooms.

Then, in 1962, prayer was officially removed from public schools. This was followed in 1963 by making unconstitutional Bible reading in public schools, stating, *"If portions of the New Testament were read without explanation, the could and have been psychologically harmful to children."* In 1965 the court denied a student the right in a public school cafeteria to bow his or her head and offer

---

1. Wieseltier, "Washington Diarist," 34.

prayer. In 1980, the Ten Commandments were outlawed in schools. The court said, "If the posted copies of the Ten Commandments wee to have any effect at all, it would be to induce school children to read them. And if they read them, meditated upon them, and perhaps venerated them, this is not a permissible objective.

Since that time copies of the Ten Commandments can no longer be displayed on the property of any government building, whether local, county, state or federal! What is next? Erasing from our money any reference to God? Chiseling any reference to God and the Bible from all public monuments? Limiting the activity of churches? Removing their tax-except status? Our counts have set us on a course of moral and spiritual shipwreck. Revisionists have purged out history books of references to faith in and dependence on God. Is this what we want for our nation, founded as it was on Christian principles?

While these limitations are going on, Islam is granted special privileges. In some public schools, Islam is taught as an important religion. In Times Square in New York City, on certain special Islamic holy days, the square is cordoned off, so that thousands of Muslims may kneel publicly in prayer. Are we only separating church and state in the case of Christianity?

CONCLUSION

The struggle for religious freedom "has become our heritage after long centuries of struggle and human suffering."[2] On June 17, 1825, in his address at the Bunker Hill monument,

2. Tolle, *Religious Freedom*, 4.

Daniel Webster said, *"If the true spark of religious and civil liberty be kindled, it will burn."*

Historically, the Supreme Court refrained from infringing on freedom of religion. More recently, it has come to limit religious freedom through its decisions. It is my prayer that it will reverse its current trend and that we will all continue to keep the spark of religious liberty kindled, so that it will continue to burn brightly.

Chapter 13

References to God on Our National Seal and Monuments

WRITTEN IN stone—the message that God is recognized by our nation is found on the surfaces of our national monuments. Some of these are very visible, while others may not be so, but all are there to contemplate.

WASHINGTON MONUMENT

"'*Laus Deo*,' which is Latin for 'Praise be to God,' ... is on the east side of the 100-ounce aluminum cap of the Washington Monument."[1] A replica of the monument's cap is on display at American Christian Heritage, under the National Park Service's directorship.

"Since the actual inscription on the cap, which on the other three sides provides other information, is not viewable atop the 555-foot stone column, the National Park Service has created a replica, which is on display inside the white-colored obelisk of marble, granite and sandstone."[2]

However, the replica has been placed in such a way as to make it impossible to see the east side of it. Todd

---

1. Unruh, "God banished."
2. Ibid.

DuBord, a California minister, has noticed this on various visits to the monument and has commented on it.

"'Surely, I thought, if the one side of the replica is hidden from public sight, they have certainly written something about it,' he continued. However, 'There was no description of "Laus Deo" on the front side of the replica stand. There was also no description of "Laus Deo" on the large information display on the wall in back of the replica. There was nothing there, absolutely nothing—no way for any visitor to ever know that the words, 'Laus Deo,' . . . were inscribed on the original cap!'"[3] At the 140 ft. landing of the monument is a stone inscribed with a prayer from the City of Baltimore. At the 260 ft. landing are numerous stones quoting the Bible. A copy of the Bible is sealed in the monument's cornerstone.

LINCOLN MEMORIAL

On the walls of this monument are engraved Lincoln's Gettysburg address and Second Inaugural Address, both of which refer to God and Divine Guidance.

The latter address includes a quote from Matthew 18:7. It also has this inscribed message from the Bible: "*The Judgments of the Lord are righteous.*"

JEFFERSON MEMORIAL

Quotes from the Declaration of Independence portray Jefferson's view of deity and divine guidance. His statements from the *Virginia Statute for Religious Freedom* and

---

3. Unruh, "Now, God banished from *Washington Monument*," WorldNetDaily

Notes of the State of Virginia reflect his reliance on God. In this latter document we find these words: *"God who gave us life gave us liberty. Can the liberties of a nation be secure when we have removed the conviction that these liberties are the gift of God?"* How, indeed?

LIBRARY OF CONGRESS

On the ceiling and walls of the Library of Congress are Bible quotations. These include *"The light shineth in darkness and the darkness comprehendeth it not"* (John 1:5), and *"Wisdom is the principle thing; therefore get wisdom . . . "* (Prov 4:7).

Statues and quotes adorn the Main Reading Room. Moses and Paul represent Religion and are accompanied by the inscription, *"What doth the Lord require of thee but to do justly, to love mercy and to walk humbly with thy God"* (Micah 6:8). Science has this quote: *"The heavens declare the glory of God; and the firmament showeth his handiwork"* (Psalm 19:1). Science is represented by this statement: *"One God, one law, one element and one far-off divine event, to which the whole creation moves."*

LIBERTY BELL

The inscription on the Liberty Bell at Independence Hall in Philadelphia is a direct quote from Leviticus 25:10: *"Proclaim liberty throughout the land unto all the inhabitants thereof."*

WHITE HOUSE

John Adams, the first resident of the White House, had this inscription placed on the fireplace in the State Dining Room: *"I Pray Heaven to bestow the best of Blessings on this house and on all that hereafter shall inhabit it. May none but Honest and Wise men ever rule under this Roof."*

U.S. CAPITOL

The Capitol Building has among its inscriptions the following:

> *"America! God shed his grace on Thee, and crown thy good with brotherhood from sea to shining sea!"*
> —Katharine Lee Bates
> ("America the Beautiful").

> *Whenever a people or an institution forget its hard beginnings, it is beginning to decay."*
> —Carl Sandburg.
> (Cox Corridor, U.S. Capitol).

There are eight large paintings in the Rotunda, each depicting some aspect of our largely Christian heritage. These include:

- The baptism of Pocahontas, the first recorded conversion to the Christian faith in the American colonies.
- The Pilgrims' prayerful departure from Holland to the New World.

A carved relief in the Rotunda pictures William Penn's treaty with the Indians. He called his colony a *"holy experiment, one given to him by God."*[4]

Another relief shows the Pilgrims' landing. Their avowed purpose had been "for the Glory of God, and Advancement of the Christian Faith."[5]

SENATE CHAMBER

Over the east doorway is the Òatin phrase, *"Annuit coeptis"* (God has favored our undertakings). Over the south entrance is inscribed, *"In God we trust."*

HOUSE CHAMBER

Above the speaker's rostrum in the House Chamber is engraved our nation's motto, *"In God We Trust."* Also in the chamber is a large carving of Moses, God's ancient lawgiver.

Throughout the capitol are statues of great American leaders, many of whom were preachers. Two of these are Roger Williams and Marcus Whitman.

PRAYER ROOM

Yes, the Capitol has a prayer room and in it a stained glass window showing George Washington, an open Bible and the following inscription:

"Preserve me, O God: for in thee do I put my trust" (Psalm 16:1).

4. Yoder, from a paper in a series by the Joan B. Kroc Institute for International Peace Studies, 2011

5. Mayflower Compact, November 11, 1620

IN GOD WE TRUST ... OR DO WE?

SUPREME COURT BUILDING

"Every argument before the U.S. Supreme Court and every opinion the justices deliver comes in the presence of the Ten Commandments, God's law given to Moses on a fire-scorched mountain, and now represented for the United States in the very artwork carved into the high court structure.

"In today's world of revisionist history, the proof comes through the work of a California pastor who visited the Supreme Court building recently when he was in Washington and was surprised that what the tour guides were telling him wasn't the same thing as what he was seeing. They explained that the Roman numerals I to X referred to the first Ten Amendments and not to the Ten Commandments. There are six depictions of Moses and/or the Ten Commandments on or in the Supreme Court Building."[6]

Engraved on the doors leading to the Judges' Chamber, there are ten Roman numerals representing the Ten Commandments. Guides explain these symbols as representing the first Ten Amendments to the Constitution, rather than to the Ten Commandments.

As you walk up the steps to the building which houses the U.S. Supreme Court you can see near the top of the building a row of the world's law givers and each one is facing one in the middle who is facing forward with a full frontal view. It is Moses and he is holding the Ten Commandments! As you enter the Supreme Court courtroom, the two doors have the Ten Commandments engraved on the lower portion of each door. As you sit inside the courtroom, you can see on the wall, right above where the Supreme Court judges

---

6. Unruh, "Stunner."

sit, a display of the Ten Commandments! There are Bible verses etched in stone all over the Federal Buildings and Monuments in Washington, DC.

Isn't this ironic? Six references to Moses and/or the Ten Commandments in the Supreme Court Building, yet a local state, county or city, or even public school, cannot have a depiction of the Ten Commandments. Again, anyone for consistency?

NATIONAL ARCHIVES

On the floor of the Rotunda is a depiction of the Ten Commandments. The archives house the two most important documents of our history—The Declaration of Independence and The Constitution. Both of these documents underscore biblical principles.

INSCRIPTION ON THE TOMB OF THE UNKNOWNS

On the monument formerly known as the Tomb of the Unknown Soldier, is this inscription:

"Here Rests In Honored Glory An American Soldier Known But To God."

Is this a government monument, guarded by military personnel? Certainly. Then note that the remains of soldiers interred in the tomb are understood to be under God's care and recognition.

OUR NATIONAL SEAL

The Latin words *Annuit Coeptus* on the seal mean, "Providence has favored our undertaking."

GOD ON OUR MONEY

Despite continued efforts by those who want to expunge references to God from all official documents, I just now looked at some coins and bills and found *"In God we trust"* on every one of them. This is government-issued and sanctioned currency, yet it has God's name still emblazoned on it. At the highest levels, again of our government, dependence on God is noted. Perhaps at no level is this more important than at that of our money. In God do we trust, or is it in monetary matters do we trust? Our government tells us that our trust should be in God. This slogan comes from the statement to that effect in our national anthem:

> "And this be our motto: 'In God is our trust.'
> And the Star Spangled Banner in triumph shall wave
> O'er the land of the free and the home of the brave."

In 1864, the words were shortened to "In God We Trust" and applied to a newly designed two-cent coin.

Religious Tolerance, an organization aimed at defending the freedom of all religions, notes,

"Almost a century and a half ago, eleven Protestant denominations mounted a campaign to add references to God to the U.S. Constitution and other federal documents. Rev. M.R. Watkinson of Ridleyville, Penn., was the first of many to write a letter to the Secretary of the Treasury Salmon P. Chase in 1861 to promote this concept. Watkinson suggested the words, '*God, Liberty, Law*.' In 1863, Chase asked the Director of the Mint, James Pollock, to prepare suitable wording '*God Our Trust.*' Chase picked '*In God We Trust*' to be used on some of the government's coins. The phrase was a subtle reminder that the Union considered itself on God's side with respect to slavery. Congress passed enabling legislation. Since an 1837 Act of Congress specified the mottos and devices that were to be placed on U.S. coins, it was necessary to pass another act to enable the motto to be added. This was done by means of 1886-APR-22. The motto has been in use on the one-cent coin since 1909, and on the ten-cent coin since 1916."[7]

Theodore Roosevelt disapproved of the motto. In a letter to William Boldly November 11, 1907, he wrote:

"*My own feeling in the matter is due to my very firm conviction that to put such a motto on coins, or to use it in any kindred manner, not only does no good but does positive harm, and is in effect irreverence, which comes dangerously close to sacrilege . . . It is a motto which it is indeed well to have inscribed on our great national monuments, in our temples of justice, in our legislative halls, and in building such as those at West Point and Annapolis—in short, wherever it will tend to arouse and inspire a lofty emotion in those who look thereon. But it seems to me eminently unwise to cheapen such a motto by use on coins, just as it would be to cheapen it by use on postage stamps, or in advertisements.*"[8]

In 1956, the nation was suffering through the Cold War, and the McCarthy Communist witch hunt. Partly in reaction to these factors, the eighty-fourth Congress

7. www.religious tolerance.org, July 1997.
8. Cited in Schwarz 1976, 76.

passed a joint resolution to replace the existing motto with "*In God We Trust*." The president signed the resolution into law July 30, 1956. The change was partly motivated by a desire to differentiate between communism, which was atheistic, and Western democracies, which were at least nominally Christian."[9]

OTHER EXAMPLES IN OUR GOVERNMENT'S STRUCTURES AND DOCUMENTS

Photojournalist Carrie Devorah took pictures of religious images in government "Some U.S. stamps have religious themes. Will the courts eventually outlaw these images, as they have other religious symbols, such as former Alabama Chief Justice Roy Moore's Ten Commandments monument? If not, why not?"[10]

Other photos in her series: (1) Jesuit Father James Marquette in the U.S. Capitol; (2) Inscription inside the Washington Monument; (3) Sculpture in front of the U.S. district court building; (4) Image called "Religion" in the U.S. Capitol; (5) Carving of the Ten Commandments on doors of the U.S. Supreme Court; (6) Charlemagne inside U.S. Supreme Court; (7) Muhammad inside U.S. Supreme Court; (8) Painting in U.S. Capitol of Pocahontas' baptism; (9) Three U.S. stamps commemorating religious holidays; (10) Discovery of the Mississippi River by Hernando De Soto in the U.S. Capitol; (11) Christmas tree in the Library of Congress with detail of one of its ornaments.

9. religioustolerance.org, July 1997.
10. *God in the Temples of Government II*, 2003.

To this list we should add the annual Christmas tree on the White House lawn. The White House is government property, yet it sports a very imposing decorated tree each Christmas season. If that can be done with impunity, why cannot Christmas symbols be permitted on other federal, state, county or city property?

CONCLUSION

References to God and Bible characters are found engraved in stone on many national buildings and monuments. These stones cry out! They tell us that our forebears in government believed in God and were not averse to making their faith public on our monuments. Of course, this implies that, in the case of our federal government, there is no strict separation between church and state. Therefore, if federal properties in Washington, DC, are replete with Christian symbols, why cannot state and local governments include Christian symbols on their property? Why must a city government be forced to remove a Ten Commandments monument from its grounds? Answer me that, federal judges!

Chapter 14

God in Our Pledge of Allegiance, Oaths of Office

ALTHOUGH CONTINUAL efforts are being made to force God out of our Pledge of Allegiance, He is still there. He is still in our federal oaths of office. He is still there on our money. The deniers of our faith-based history have not yet succeeded in expunging the name of God from our oaths and documents, and I pray that they never will. Read below:

THE PLEDGE OF ALLEGIANCE

This pledge "is an oath of loyalty to the republic of the United States, composed by Francis Bellamy in 1892. The Pledge has been modified four times since then, with the most recent change adding the words "under God" in 1954."[1] The Pledge is predominantly sworn by children in public schools in response to laws in many states requiring the Pledge to be offered. Congressional sessions open with the swearing of the Pledge, as do government meetings at

---

1. Wikipedia, "Pledge of Allegiance."

local levels, meetings held by the Boy Scouts of America, and some sporting events.[2]

The current version of the Pledge of Allegiance reads:

"I pledge allegiance to the flag of the United States of America, and to the Republic for which it stands, one Nation under God, indivisible, with liberty and justice for all."

"Under God" has been a bone of legal contention ever since it was added to the pledge in 1954. Why should it not be included? Is it not in the spirit of all of the documents we have examined from our history as a nation?

OATHS OF OFFICE

President-elect Barack Obama used the Bible on which Abraham Lincoln took the presidential oath in 1861. Chief Justice Roberts concluded the oath by adding, *"So help you God?"* And Obama, following a practice established by George Washington and followed by most of our presidents, replied: *"So help me God."*

On August 8, 2009, Sonia Sotomayor was sworn in as a justice of the U.S. Supreme Court. She placed her hand on a Bible as she took the oath of office, adding, *"So help me God."*

CONCLUSION

Does this mean that there is an absolute separation between church and state, or is there a mixing of the two in high government circles? Officials down the chain of authority, however, are not permitted to mix the two. Local

2. Ibid.

governments cannot do so. Schools cannot have official prayers. Yet, the Supreme Court invokes God in its oaths of office and opens its sessions with prayer. Again, is there not something highly inconsistent in all of this?

Actually, the concept of separation between church and state is not found in any founding document of our nation. It appeared for the first time in that notorious letter written by Thomas Jefferson, in which he declared that *"there is a high wall of separation between church and state."* Yet, as we have seen, he invoked God in public statements. His letter, never a government document, for some strange reason has become the official dogma of the Supreme Court and lesser courts.

Chapter 15

God in Our National Anthem and Hymns

OUT OF the depths of his heart, as he spent the night aboard a British warship, hearing and watching the British bombardment going on against Fort McHenry, near Baltimore, Francis Scott Key agonized for his country. He was helpless to intervene, so could only await the next morning, to see if the fort had survived. What he saw at dawn was the Stars and Stripes still flying over an unbowed fort. This so moved him that he wrote a poem about it. This poem eventually became our National Anthem.

THE STAR-SPANGLED BANNER[1]

Following is the final verse of *The Star Spangled Banner*, made officially our national anthem in 1931. It is almost never sung or even remembered, but makes a strong statement about our dependence as a nation upon God.

> *O, thus be it ever when freemen shall stand,*
> *Between their lov'd homes and the war's desolation;*
> *Blest with vict'ry and peace, may the heav'n-rescued land*
> *Praise the Pow'r that hath made and preserv'd us a nation!*
> *Then conquer we must, when our cause is just,*
> *And this be our motto: "In God is our trust."*

1. Francis Scott Key, 1814.

*And the star-spangled banner in triumph shall wave
O'er the land of the free and the home of the brave!*

THE NATIONAL HYMN[2]

*God of our fathers, whose almighty hand
Leads forth in beauty all the starry band
Of shining worlds in splendor through the skies
Our grateful songs before Thy throne arise.
Thy love divine hath led us in the past,
In this free land by Thee our lot is cast,
Be Thou our Ruler, Guardian, Guide and Stay,
Thy Word our law, Thy paths our chosen way.
From war's alarms, from deadly pestilence,
Be Thy strong arm our ever sure defense;
Thy true religion in our hearts increase,
Thy bounteous goodness nourish us in peace.
Refresh Thy people on their toilsome way,
Lead us from night to never ending day;
Fill all our lives with love and grace divine,
And glory, laud, and praise be ever Thine.*

AMERICA—MY COUNTRY 'TIS OF THEE[3]

*My country, 'tis of thee,
sweet land of liberty, of thee I sing;
land where my fathers died,
land of the pilgrims' pride,*

---

2. Words by Daniel Roberts, 1876; music by George W. Warren, 1888.

3. Text by Samuel F. Smith, 1832; music in *Thesaurus Musicus*. The writer of this music, "God Save the Queen," is unknown.

from every mountainside let freedom ring!
My native country, thee,
land of the noble free, thy name I love;
I love thy rocks and rills,
thy woods and templed hills;
my heart with rapture thrills, like that above.
Let music swell the breeze,
and ring from all the trees sweet freedom's song;
let mortal tongues awake;
let all that breathe partake;
let rocks their silence break, the sound prolong.
Our fathers' God, to thee,
author of liberty, to thee we sing;
long may our land be bright
with freedom's holy light;
protect us by thy might,
great God, our King.

AMERICA THE BEAUTIFUL[4]

O beautiful for spacious skies,
For amber waves of grain,
For purple mountain majesties
Above the fruited plain!
America! America!
God shed his grace on thee
And crown thy good with brotherhood
From sea to shining sea!
O beautiful for pilgrim feet
Whose stern impassioned stress

---

4. Words by Katharine Lee Bates, 1895; melody by Samuel Ward, 1892.

*A thoroughfare of freedom beat
Across the wilderness!
America! America!
God mend thine every flaw,
Confirm thy soul in self-control,
Thy liberty in law!
O beautiful for heroes proved
In liberating strife.
Who more than self their country loved
And mercy more than life!
America! America!
May God thy gold refine
Till all success be nobleness
And every gain divine!
O beautiful for patriot dream
That sees beyond the years
Thine alabaster cities gleam
Undimmed by human tears!
America! America!
God shed his grace on thee
And crown thy good with brotherhood
From sea to shining sea!
O beautiful for halcyon skies,
For amber waves of grain,
For purple mountain majesties
Above the enameled plain!
America! America!
God shed his grace on thee
Till souls wax fair as earth and air
And music-hearted sea!
O beautiful for pilgrims' feet,
Whose stem impassioned stress
A thoroughfare for freedom beat
Across the wilderness!*

America! America!
God shed his grace on thee
Till paths be wrought through
wilds of thought
By pilgrim foot and knee!
O beautiful for glory-tale
Of liberating strife
When once and twice,
for man's avail
Men lavished precious life!
America! America!
God shed his grace on thee
Till selfish gain no longer stain
The banner of the free!
O beautiful for patriot dream
That sees beyond the years
Thine alabaster cities gleam
Undimmed by human tears!
America! America!
God shed his grace on thee
Till nobler men keep once again
Thy whiter jubilee!

BATTLE HYMN OF THE REPUBLIC[5]

This poem was perhaps the best-known Civil War song of the Union Army, and is now a well-loved American patriotic anthem.

> *Mine eyes have seen the glory of the coming of the Lord:*
> *He is trampling out the vintage where the grapes of wrath are stored;*

---

5. Words by Julia Ward Howe, 1862, sung to an American folk melody.

He hath loosed the fateful lightning of His terrible swift sword:
His truth is marching on.

I have seen Him in the watch-fires of a hundred circling camps,
They have builded Him an altar in the evening dews and damps;
I can read His righteous sentence by the dim and flaring lamps:
His day is marching on.
I have read a fiery gospel writ in burnished rows of steel:
"As ye deal with my contemners, so with you my grace shall deal;
Let the Hero, born of woman, crush the serpent with his heel,
Since God is marching on."
He has sounded forth the trumpet that shall never call retreat;
He is sifting out the hearts of men before His judgment-seat:
Oh, be swift, my soul, to answer Him! be jubilant, my feet!
Our God is marching on.
In the beauty of the lilies Christ was born across the sea,
With a glory in his bosom that transfigures you and me:
As he died to make men holy, let us die to make men free,
While God is marching on.

GOD BLESS AMERICA[6]

(An excerpt)

God Bless America,
Land that I love.
Stand beside her, and guide her
Thru the night with a light from above.
From the mountains, to the prairies,
To the oceans, white with foam
God bless America, My home sweet home.

---

6. Words and music by Irving Berlin, 1938–1939.

ETERNAL FATHER, STRONG TO SAVE —THE NAVY HYMN[7]

Eternal Father, Strong to save,
Whose arm hath bound the restless wave,
Who bid'st the mighty Ocean deep
Its own appointed limits keep;
O hear us when we cry to thee,
For those in peril on the sea.
O Christ! Whose voice the waters heard
And hushed their raging at Thy word,
Who walked'st on the foaming deep,
and calm amidst its rage didst sleep;
Oh hear us when we cry to Thee
For those in peril on the sea!
Most Holy Spirit! Who didst brood
Upon the chaos dark and rude,
And bid its angry tumult cease,
And give, for wild confusion, peace;
Oh, hear us when we cry to Thee
For those in peril on the sea!

O Trinity of love and power!
Our brethren shield in danger's hour;
From rock and tempest, fire and foe,
Protect them wheresoe'er they go;
Thus evermore shall rise to Thee,
Glad hymns of praise from land and sea.

In the United States, "in 1879 Rear Adm. Charles Jackson Train, an 1865 graduate of the United States Naval

---

7. William Whiting, 1860, and John B. Dykes, 1861. Text taken from a publication of the Bureau of Naval Personnel, Naval Historical Center, Washington, DC, n.d.

Academy at Annapolis, was a lieutenant commander stationed at the Academy in charge of the Midshipman Choir. In that year, Lt. Comdr. Train inaugurated the present practice of concluding each Sunday's divine services at the academy with the singing of the first verse of this hymn."[8]

"This hymn is often used at funerals for personnel who served in or were associated with the Navy. "Eternal Father" was the favorite hymn of President Franklin D. Roosevelt and was sung at his funeral at Hyde Park, New York, in April, 1945. Roosevelt had served as Secretary of the Navy. This hymn was also played as President John F. Kennedy's body was carried up the steps of the capitol to lie in state"[9]

CONCLUSION: WHAT TO NOTE IN THESE ANTHEMS

In every one of these patriotic songs we see mention of God, from Francis Scott Key's poem in 1814, which became our national anthem, to Irving Berlin's great song, *God Bless America*. We not only have countless documents in our history proclaiming faith in God, but also references to him in our monuments, our national anthems and hymns, and our poetry. Who can doubt that our nation was initiated, grew and still grows on faith in Divine Providence to guide us?

---

8. The United States Navy Historical Archives. Although written by two English clerics, this hymn became the recognized anthem of the U.S. Navy. Its story is found on the web in the Naval Historical Center Archives, Washington, DC.

9. Ibid.

Chapter 16

References to God in Poetry by Famous (and One Not Famous) Americans

Nor to be outdone by the authors of our patriotic hymns, poets throughout our history have expressed their faith in God. Some of these follow:

FLOWER GOD, GOD OF THE SPRING

Robert Louis Stevenson

Flower god, god of the spring, beautiful, bountiful,
Cold-dyed shield in the sky, lover of versicles,
Here I wander in April
Cold, grey-headed; and still to my
Heart, Spring comes with a bound, Spring the deliverer,
Spring, song-leader in woods, chorally resonant;
Spring, flower-planter in meadows,
Child-conductor in willowy
Fields deep dotted with bloom, daisies and crocuses:
Here that child from his heart drinks of eternity:
O child, happy are children!
She still smiles on their innocence,
She, dear mother in God, fostering violets,
Fills earth full of her scents, voices and violins:

Thus one cunning in music
Wakes old chords in the memory:
Thus fair earth in the Spring leads her performances.
One more touch of the bow, smell of the virginal
Green - one more, and my bosom
Feels new life with an ecstasy.

FOUR THINGS

Henry Van Dyke, 1852–1933

Four things a man must learn to do
If he would make his record true:
To think without confusion clearly;
To love his fellow man sincerely;
To act from honest motives purely;
To trust in God and Heaven securely.

CHRIST OF EVERYWHERE

Henry Van Dyke

"Christ of the Andes," Christ of Everywhere,
Great lover of the hills, the open air,
And patient lover of impatient men
Who blindly strive and sin and strive again—
Thou Living Word, larger than any creed,
Thou Love Divine, uttered in human deed—
Oh, teach the world, warring and wandering still,
Thy way of Peace, the footpath of Good Will!

HYMN TO JOY

Henry Van Dyke, 1908, to a Beethoven tune, 1824

Joyful, joyful we adore Thee, God of glory, Lord of love,
Hearts unfold like flowers before Thee, hail Thee as the sun above.
Melt the clouds of sin and sadness, drive the dark of doubt away;
Giver of immortal gladness, fill us with the light of day.
All Thy works with joy surround Thee, earth and heav'n reflect Thy rays,
Stars and angels sing around Thee, center of unbroken praise;
Field and forest, vale and mountain, flow'ry meadow, flashing sea,
Chanting birds and flowing fountain call us to rejoice in Thee.
Thou art giving and forgiving, ever blessing, ever blest,
Wellspring of the joy of living, ocean depth of happy rest.
Thou our Father, Christ our Brother, all who live in love are Thine;
Teach us how to love each other, lift us to the Joy Divine.
Mortals, join the mighty chorus which the morning stars began,
Father love is reigning o'er us, brother love binds man to man.
Ever singing, march we onward, victors in the midst of strife;
Joyful music lifts us sunward, in the triumph song of life.

GOD'S ACRE

Henry Wadsworth Longfellow, 1807–1882

I like that ancient Saxon phrase, which calls

The burial-ground God's Acre! It is just;
It consecrates each grave within its walls,
And breathes a benison o'er the sleeping dust.
God's Acre! Yes, that blessed name imparts
Comfort to those, who in the grave have sown
The seed that they had garnered in their hearts,
Their bread of life, alas! no more their own.
Into its furrows shall we all be cast,
In the sure faith, that we shall rise again
At the great harvest, when the archangel's blast
Shall winnow, like a fan, the chaff and grain.
Then shall the good stand in immortal bloom,
In the fair gardens of that second birth;
And each bright blossom mingle its perfume
With that of flowers, which never bloomed on earth.
With thy rude ploughshare, Death, turn up the sod,
And spread the furrow for the seed we sow;
This is the field and Acre of our God,
This is the place where human harvests grow!

CHRISTMAS BELLS

Henry Wadsworth Longfellow, 1807–1882

I heard the bells on Christmas Day
Their old familiar carols play,
And wild and sweet
The words repeat
Of peace on earth, good-will to men!
And thought how, as the day had come,
The belfries of all Christendom

Had rolled along
The unbroken song
Of peace on earth, good-will to men!
Till, ringing, singing on its way,
The world revolved from night to day,
A voice, a chime
A chant sublime
Of peace on earth, good-will to men!
Then from each black accursed mouth
The cannon thundered in the South,
And with the sound
The carols drowned
Of peace on earth, good-will to men!
It was as if an earthquake rent
The hearth-stones of a continent,
And made forlorn
The households born
Of peace on earth, good-will to men!
And in despair I bowed my head;
"There is no peace on earth," I said;
"For hate is strong,
And mocks the song
Of peace on earth, good-will to men!"
Then pealed the bells more loud and deep:
"God is not dead; nor doth he sleep!
The Wrong shall fail,
The Right prevail,
With peace on earth, good-will to men!"

SAIL ON, O SHIP OF STATE

Henry Wadsworth Longfellow

Thou, too, sail on, O Ship of State!
Sail on, O Union, strong and great,
Humanity with all its fears,
With all the hopes of future years,
Is hanging breathless on thy fate!
We know what Master laid thy keel . . .

A PSALM OF LIFE

Henry Wadsworth Longfellow

Tell me not, in mournful numbers,
Life is but an empty dream!—
For the soul is dead that slumbers,
And things are not what they seem.
Life is real! Life is earnest!
And the grave is not its goal;
Dust thou art, to dust returnest,
Was not spoken of the soul.
Not enjoyment, and not sorrow,
Is our destined end or way;
But to act, that each tomorrow
Find us farther than today.
Art is long, and Time is fleeting,
And our hearts, though stout and brave,
Still, like muffled drums, are beating
Funeral marches to the grave.
In the world's broad field of battle,

In the bivouac of Life,
Be not dumb, driven cattle!
Be a hero in the strife!
Trust no Future, howe'er pleasant!
Let the dead Past bury its dead!
Act,—act in the living Present!
Heart within, and God o'erhead!
Lives of great men all remind us
We can make our lives sublime,
And, departing, leave behind us
Footprints in the sands of time;
Footprints, that perhaps another,
Sailing o'er life's solemn main,
A forlorn and shipwrecked brother,
Seeing, shall take heart again.
Let us, then, be up and doing,
With a heart for any fate;
Still achieving, still pursuing,
Learn to labor and to wait.

JOHN GREENLEAF WHITTIER, 1807–1892

Before me, even as behind, God is, and all is well.
Beauty seen is never lost, God's colors all are fast.

DEAR LORD AND FATHER OF MANKIND

John Greenleaf Whittier, 1807–1892

Dear Lord and Father of mankind,
Forgive our foolish ways;
Reclothe us in our rightful mind,

In purer lives Thy service find,
In deeper reverence, praise.
In simple trust like theirs who heard,
Beside the Syrian Sea,
The gracious calling of the Lord,
Let us, like them, without a word,
Rise up and follow Thee.
O Sabbath rest by Galilee,
O calm of hills above,
Where Jesus knelt to share with thee
The silence of eternity
Interpreted by love!
Drop thy still dews of quietness,
Till all our strivings cease;
Take from our souls the strain and stress,
And let our ordered lives confess
The beauty of thy peace.

GOD'S WORLD

Edna St. Vincent Millay, 1892–1950

O world, I cannot hold thee close enough! Thy winds, thy wide grey skies! Thy mists that roll and rise! Thy woods, this autumn day, that ache and sag And all but cry with colour! That gaunt crag to crush! To lift the lean of that black bluff! World, World, I cannot get thee close enough! Long have I known a glory in it all, But never knew I this; Here such a passion is As stretcheth me apart. Lord, I do fear Thou'st made the world too beautiful this year. My soul is all but out of me, let fall No burning leaf; prithee, let no bird call.

WHAT DO I LIKE ABOUT THIS COUNTRY?

Glover Shipp

In honor of 9/11

What do I like about this country?
What do I like about this land?
Lofty snow-draped mountains
And oceans' crystal strands.
Rock-ribbed canyons winding
And verdant forest stands.
Farms and ranches stretching;
O'er plains they stamp their brand.
Bustling cities rising,
Their spires proudly planned.
What do I like about this country?
What do I like about this land?
People of all backgrounds
From ev'ry tribe and clan;
Ev'ry tongue and culture,
United hand-to-hand.
Freedom's flame ignited
By patriots' noble band,
Its fire unquenched forever,
All luminous and grand.
What do I like about this country?
What do I like about this land?
Here we plant our banner
And here, our flag's broad bands.
Here we fight for freedom
And here we take our stand—

Worship freely lifted
By loving hearts and hands.
Praise to God eternal,
Who blesses all our land.

CONCLUSION

Great poets in our history also weighed in on spiritual values. Some of our best poems and hymns were written by God-fearing and patriotic American poets, whose words still resonate in our hearts.

Chapter 17

Quotes from Famous Americans on God and the Bible

IF WE were to include in this chapter every quote by American figures about God and the Bible, it would be far too long to be practical. For this reason we include a representative number from different periods of our history.

PATRICK HENRY, 1765, SPEECH TO THE HOUSE OF BURGESSES

"It cannot be emphasized too clearly and too often that this nation was founded, not by religionists, but by Christians; not on religion, but on the gospel of Jesus Christ. For this very reason, peoples of other faiths have been afforded asylum, prosperity, and freedom of worship here."

BENJAMIN RUSH, IN DENOUNCING THE TEA ACT, 1775

"What shining examples of patriotism do we behold in Joshua, Samuel, Maccabees and all the illustrious princes, captains and prophets among the Jews."

JAMES MADISON, 1778, TO THE GENERAL ASSEMBLY OF THE STATE OF VIRGINIA

"We have staked the whole future of American civilization, not upon the power of government, far from it. We've staked the future of all our political institutions upon our capacity ... to sustain ourselves according to the Ten Commandments of God."

JOHN JAY, THE FIRST CHIEF JUSTICE OF THE SUPREME COURT AND AN AUTHOR OF THE LANDMARK "FEDERALIST PAPERS"

"Providence has given to our people the choice of their rulers—and it is the duty, as well as the privilege and interest of our Christian nation—to select and prefer Christians for their rulers."

GEORGE WASHINGTON

"... reason and experience both forbid us to expect, that national morality can prevail in exclusion of religious principle ..."

During the Revolutionary War, Washington lobbied Congress to maintain at least one clergyman for every two regiments.

GEORGE WASHINGTON, 1781

After the surrender at Yorktown, Washington wrote to the president of Congress: *"I take particular pleasure in acknowledging that the interposing hand of Heaven ... has* been most conspicuous and remarkable." He declared the day after the surrender to be a day of thanksgiving, and his troops were directed to attend religious services.

THOMAS JEFFERSON, 1781[1]

"God who gave us life gave us liberty. And can the liberties of a nation be thought secure when we have removed their only firm basis, a conviction in the minds of the people that these liberties are a gift from God? That they are not to be violated but with His wrath? Indeed I tremble for my country when I reflect that God is just, and that His justice cannot sleep forever."

BENJAMIN FRANKLIN, CONSTITUTIONAL CONVENTION OF 1787

"God governs in the affairs of man. And if a sparrow cannot fall to the ground without his notice, is it probable that an empire can rise without His aid? We have been assured in the Sacred Writings that except the Lord build the house, they labor in vain that build it. I firmly believe this. I also believe that, without His concurring aid, we shall succeed in this political building no better than the builders of Babel."

"I therefore beg leave to move that henceforth prayers imploring the assistance of Heaven and its blessings on our deliberations be held in this assembly every morning before we proceed to business."

---

1. Thomas Jefferson. Inscription on the northeast quadrant of the Jefferson Memorial, Washington, D.C.

This proposal was adopted in 1789. Paid chaplains were appointed for each house of Congress. This practice still continues, with prayer offered before each meeting of Congress. In addition, when the government moved to Washington, DC, Christian worship took place, not only in Congress, but also in the Supreme Court and the War and Treasury building.

ALEXANDER HAMILTON, 1787

"For my own part, I sincerely esteem it [the Constitution] a system which without the finger of God, never could have been suggested and agreed upon by such a diversity of interests."

GEORGE WASHINGTON, 1797, LETTER TO JOHN ADAMS

"Although guided by our excellent Constitution in the discharge of official duties, and actuated, through the whole course of my public life, solely by a wish to promote the best interests of our country; yet, without the beneficial interposition of the Supreme Ruler of the Universe, we could not have reached the distinguished situation which we have attained with such unprecedented rapidity. To Him, therefore, should we bow with gratitude and reverence, and endeavor to merit a continuance of His special favors."

JOHN ADAMS, 1798

"We have no government armed with power capable of contending with human passions unbridled by morality and religion. Avarice, ambition, revenge, or gallantry, would

break the strongest cords of our Constitution as a whale goes through a net. Our Constitution was made only for a moral and religious people. It is wholly inadequate to the government of any other."

"Suppose a nation in some distant region should take the Bible for their only law book, and every member should regulate his conduct by the precepts there exhibited! Every member would be obliged by conscience to temperance, frugality, and industry; to justice, kindness, and charity towards his fellow men; and to piety, love, and reverence toward Almighty God . . . What a Utopia, what a Paradise would this region be."

"Statesmen may plan and speculate for liberty, but it is religion and morality which can establish the principles upon which freedom can securely stand."

CHARLES CARROLL, SIGNER OF THE DECLARATION OF INDEPENDENCE, TO JAMES MCHENRY, 1800

"Without morals a republic cannot subsist any length of time; they therefore who are decrying the Christian religion, whose morality is so sublime and pure . . . are undermining the solid foundation of morals, the best security for the duration of free governments."

THOMAS PAINE, THE EXISTENCE OF GOD, 1810

"It has been the error of the schools to teach astronomy, and all the other sciences, and subjects of natural philosophy, as accomplishments only; whereas they should be taught *theologically, or with reference to the Being who is the author of them: for all the principles of science are of divine origin. Man cannot make, or invent, or contrive principles: he can only discover them; and he ought to look through the discovery to the Author."*

JOHN QUINCY ADAMS, 1816, IN A LETTER TO HIS SON

"... *you know the difference between right and wrong, and you know some of your duties, and the obligations you are under... It is in the Bible you must learn them, and from the Bible how to practice them."*

JOHN QUINCY ADAMS, 1821

"The highest glory of the American Revolution was this: It connected in one indissoluble bond the principles of civil government with the principles of Christianity."

DANIEL WEBSTER

"If the power of the Gospel is not felt through the length and breadth of the land, anarchy and misrule, degradation and misery, corruption and darkness will reign without mitigation or end."

"Let our object be our country, our whole country, and nothing but our country. And, by the blessing of God, may that country itself become a vast and splendid monument, not of possession and terror, but of wisdom, of peace, and of liberty, upon which the world may gaze with admiration."

RALPH WALDO EMERSON, 1803–1882

"God enters by a private door into every individual."

ALEXIS DE TOCQUEVILLE, 1835

And now, observations, not by an American statesman, but by a foreign historian and political scientist, Alexis de Tocqueville, after having traveled the U.S. extensively in the early decades of our national history:

". . . there is no country in the whole world in which the Christian religion retains a greater influence over the souls of men than in America; and there can be no greater proof of its utility, and of its conformity to human nature, than that its influence is most powerfully felt over the most enlightened and free nation of the earth."

ALEXIS DE TOCQUEVILLE, N.D.

"America is great because she is good. If America ceases to be good, America will cease to be great."

"The Americans combine the notions of religion and liberty so intimately in their minds, that it is impossible to make them conceive of one without the other."

PRESIDENT JAMES A. GARFIELD

"In giving you being, God locked up in your nature certain forces and capabilities. What will you do with them? . . . I implore you to cherish and guard and use well the forces that God has given to you."

GEORGE WASHINGTON CARVER

"I am simply trying as best I can and as fast as God gives me light to do the job I believe He has given me in trust to do."

FRANKLIN D. ROOSEVELT IN A 1935 RADIO ADDRESS

"We cannot read the history of our rise and development as a nation, without reckoning with the place the Bible has occupied in shaping the advances of the Republic . . . where we have been truest and most consistent in obeying its precepts, we have attained the greatest measure of contentment and prosperity."

HARRY S. TRUMAN'S MESSAGE TO CONGRESS FOLLOWING THE DEATH OF PRESIDENT ROOSEVELT

Omitted from the record on the World War II Memorial were these words:

"At this moment, I have in my heart a prayer. As I assume my heavy duties, I humbly pray to God, in the words of Solomon: 'Give therefore thy servant an understanding heart to judge thy people, that I may discern between good and bad: for who is able to judge this thy so great a people?' I ask only to be a good and faithful servant of my Lord and of my people."

Also omitted from the monument were these words from his speech on the surrender of Germany:

"We are resolute in our determination—we will see the fight through to a complete and victorious finish. To that end,

with the help of God, we shall use every ounce of our energy and strength."

GENERAL DOUGLAS MACARTHUR, ON THE SURRENDER OF JAPAN

"As I look back upon the long, tortuous trail from those grim days of Bataan and Corregidor . . . I thank a merciful God that he has given us the faith, the courage and the power from which to mold victory."

GENERAL DWIGHT D. EISENHOWER

"Without God there can be no American form of government, nor an American way of life."

Eisenhower, on adding "under God" to the Pledge of Allegiance:

"In this way we are reaffirming the transcendence of religious faith in America's heritage and future."

Omitted from the World War II Memorial record of his speech to the troops prior to D-Day, "Good luck! And let us all beseech the blessing of Almighty God upon this great and noble undertaking."

JOHN F. KENNEDY

"We in this country, in this generation, are—by destiny rather than choice—the watchmen on the walls of world freedom. We ask, therefore, that we may be worthy of our power and responsibility, that we may exercise our strength with wisdom and restraint, and that we may achieve in our time and for all time the ancient vision of 'peace on earth, good will toward men.' That must always be our goal, and the righteousness of our cause must always underlie our strength. For as was written long ago: 'Except the Lord keep the city, the watchman waketh but in vain.'"[2]

CHARLES WILLIAM ELLIOT, PRESIDENT, HARVARD UNIVERSITY

"When the universities hold up before their youth the great Semitic ideals which were embodied in the Decalogue [The Ten Commandments], they mean that these ideals should be applied in politics. When they teach their young men that Asiatic ideal . . . the Golden Rule, they mean that their disciples shall apply it to business; when they inculcate that comprehensive maxim of Christian ethics, 'Ye are all members of one another,' they mean that this moral principle is applicable to all human relations, whether between individuals, families, states or nations."

The original Harvard Handbook, 1636, read, as Rule No. 1: "Let every student be plainly instructed and earnestly pressed to consider well, the main end of his life and studies, to know God and Jesus Christ, which is eternal life."

PRESIDENT WILLIAM LAMBDIN PRATHER, TEXAS STATE UNIVERSITY (NOW THE UNIVERSITY OF TEXAS) GRADUATION, 1905

"We cannot read the sealed orders which the Creator has placed in your hands, but we breathe the prayer that in

---

2. Courtesy of the John Fitzgerald Kennedy Library, Boston, Massachusetts. This is from a speech he had prepared to give in Dallas on the day of his assassination, November 22, 1963.

victory and defeat, success and failure, you will rise in the strength of noble manhood and womanhood to meet the issues hat confront you ... In parting, let me leave with you for your encouragement, guidance and stay for all years that are to come, a sentiment which I would fain engrave upon the hearts of each one of you: 'Whoso walketh uprightly walketh surely." May the richest blessings of a kind Providence ever abide with you."

—This is from his speech as published in 1905 in a book of essays. How times have changed! Public university presidents might find it dangerous to refer to God and quote from the Bible as these educators did.

SENATOR ROBERT BYRD, DIED 2010

"... to remove God from this country will destroy it."

CONCLUSION

All of these remarks about God were from intelligent leaders of our country. Surely we cannot dismiss them as ignorant clods. Surely we must consider the possibility that they really believed and gave voice to their belief. Can we do no less?

Chapter 18

Current Voices on Faith in God

"WHEN THE *Son of Man (the Lord Jesus) comes, will He find faith on the earth?*" (Luke 18:8). The trouble is, we don't know when He will return, despite a long string of claims to the contrary. He told us, *"So you must also be ready, because the Son of Man will come at an hour when you do not expect him"* (Matt 24:44).

During this interim before the end of time is there still faith on the earth? More specifically, is there still faith among our national and state leaders? Let us quote from some contemporary voices on the sovereignty of God over our nation:

CONTEMPORARY VOICES

> "Even though the state of affairs in America today may look bleak in some respects, a gleaming ray of hope appears—God has a destiny for America! He always honors His covenants with men and our nation is based solidly on a covenant with an Almighty God. His sovereign hand is still guiding us through history."[1]

---

1. Jay Rogers, 2008, the Forerunner online magazine.

> *"We ask also today your blessings for this great nation. Even as we face challenging times, keep us ever mindful of the blessings of liberty and prosperity that you have showered upon us. May we always aspire to transcendent ideals rooted in your eternal law, and never give in to cynicism or despair. Help America always to be that "shining city on a hill," a beacon of hope to the nations"*[2]

Following the shooting November 5, 2009, at Fort Hood, Texas, in which thirteen people were killed and another thirty-eight were injured, a memorial service was held November 10 at the fort. Christian hymns were played, the base chaplain, an Evangelical Lutheran, led a prayer addressed to God and President Obama referred to faith. James Robison, Christian leader and writer, had this to say about that day:

> *"I was deeply moved as Gen. Casey referred to the Scriptures as 'God's Holy Word' and noted that these verses are read at the departure of everyone we lose in the Armed Services. From the book of Isaiah: 'Whom will I send, and who will go for us?' And of course, our soldiers answer, 'Here am I. Send me.'"*[3]

Military base? Hymns? Christian prayer? And all of this on government property! When a crisis presents itself, our leaders turn to God for help and comfort, despite what the courts may say about "separation of church and state."

---

2. (Matthew Wilson, Professor, Southern Methodist University, 2009).

3. From wordsoflife.org, message e-mailed 09-16-09.

GOD'S SOVEREIGNTY OVER NATIONS

Writing March 12, 2002, the author of Midnight Hour Ministries said this about the sovereignty of God over the affairs of nations:

> "Question: In truth can there really be a separation of church (religion) and state in the affairs of a people?
>
> "Answer: No. Why? God is the sovereign Lord over everything. Every aspect of human life comes under His jurisdiction. He is the judge of all the earth . . . No area of the life of a nation is immune to His governance. He expects that men and nations honor Him in all undertakings."

JOHN GLENN, ASTRONAUT, 1962

Through the windows of the Discovery rocket, Glenn said,

> "To look at this kind of creation out here and not believe in God is to me impossible. It just strengthens my faith. I wish there were words to describe what it is like."

NASA ASTRONAUT COL. DOUG WHEELOCK, COMMANDER OF ISS EXPEDITION 25

" . . . *I am convinced that it would require an unimaginable amount of faith to believe that all of this happened just by chance. I spent more than 20 hours outside of the Space Station on three space walks during my first mission, and the most profound sight is to view the Earth suspended in a vast, endless sea of emptiness. To me, it would be absolutely impossible to have just happened. It looks more like brush strokes from the Master's hand. It is quite surreal and profoundly breathtaking."*

ADRIAN PETERSON, RUNNING BACK WITH MINNESOTA VIKINGS

"I refocused on studying my Bible and accepting that God blessed me with this talent, and to be in this position for a reason. That reason was to reach out to others with encouraging words to help them grow."[4]

COLT MCCOY, FORMER QUARTERBACK FOR THE UNIVERSITY OF TEXAS

"My values ... keep me focused in the right direction. Without my Christian values I would just be another someone who thinks they are good because of who they are or what they have done."[5]

Many more great names could be cited, but these should suffice to show us that faith in God has been much more than the words of a lunatic fringe. They have been words from the hearts of genuine people who were not afraid to express their faith publicly.

---

4. *Distinctly Oklahoma* (December 2009) 12.
5. McMillon, "Dialogue," 22.

Chapter 19

The High Cost of Liberty

MORE THAN 230 years after the Declaration of Independence, we pretty much take our liberty for granted, including laws protecting our freedom of speech and religion. But how much has our vaunted American freedom really cost since 1776? How much did it cost to launch our nation? Apart from the more than 4,400 American patriots who died in the Revolutionary War, what did it cost the fifty-six men who signed the Declaration of Independence?

These signers were successful professional men, well educated and prosperous. Yet they boldly pledged to the cause of independence:

"For the support of this declaration, with firm reliance on the protection of divine providence, we mutually pledge to each other our lives, our fortunes and our sacred honor."

THE PRICE PAID THEIR SIGNING

Their sacred honor remained intact, but their lives and fortunes suffered severely, as was noted earlier.

THE HIGH COST OF FREEDOM CONTINUES

That was the beginning, but far from the end, of defending American liberty.

The War of 1812 soon followed, with 2,260 deaths. The Civil War was a blood bath to determine whether or not we would be a united nation. A total of 191,963 combatants on both sides died. World War I accounted for 53,402. World War II totaled 291,557. Korea accounted for 33,741 and Vietnam, 47,424. The Gulf War and Iraq have totaled 7,141, as of 2011. Afghanistan has totaled so far about 1,200. The terrifying total for all of our wars comes to more than 630,000 and counting! (National Archives and Records, US Government).

Does anyone doubt that the price tag in battle casualties alone for our freedom has been incalculable? This doesn't even include the wounded and other losses.

WORDS OF CRITICS

Yet some of our own citizens belittle all of this, as if it were nothing. Some badmouth our troops. Some ridicule our patriotism and flag-waving. Natalie Maines, of the Dixie Chicks, declared, *"Why do you have to be a patriot? About what? This land is our land. Why? . . . I don't see why people care about patriotism."*

Maines was not the first to spout such belittling words about our country and what it stands for. Richard Reid, the American citizen and notorious "shoe bomber," stated in court that his loyalty was to Osama bin Laden and Islam.

He then added, *"I think I will not apologize for my actions. I am at war with your country."*

Then, there was the story by Edward Everett Hale about Lieutenant Philip Nolan, convicted, in our early years as a nation, of treason. He answered the charge, *"Damn the United States! I wish I may never hear of the United States again."* Nolan was granted his wish, to the letter. He was condemned to spend the remainder of his life in exile on American warships. As the story goes, he repented in later years and came to love his country from afar, longing for news about her growth.

CONCLUSION

On July 4, 2011, we celebrated 235 years since our courageous Founding Fathers, men motivated in part by their faith in the Supreme Ruler of the Universe, signed their names to the Declaration of Independence. As our troops are still dying for the freedom of our nation and all others, it is appropriate to stop and thank God for them and for all of their comrades-in-arms since our nation was formed.

Chapter 20

Guarantee of Religious Freedom

IN THE United States, even from colonial days, came the concept of eventual religious freedom. Only in the colonies of Pennsylvania and Maryland, religious toleration was granted, more as an expediency than a principle. William Penn, who was a Quaker, saw to it that Pennsylvania practiced the kind of passive permission to other faiths that was the hallmark of the Quaker faith. In Maryland, Catholic Lord Baltimore saw the need for immigrants to his new colony, so invited those of various religious persuasions to settle there. He even decreed fines against those who slandered other religions.

THE SLOW PROCESS OF GAINING RELIGIOUS FREEDOM

In most of the colonies, however, there was less religious toleration. To illustrate, for a long period Virginia followed strictly the rules laid down by the Church of England. However, leaders such as Washington, Madison and Jefferson protested against any kind of state religion and infringements against conscience. In 1775 they wrote this declaration:

> "All men are equally entitled to free exercise of religion, according to the dictates of conscience, and it is mutually the duty of all to practice Christian forbearance, love, and charity toward each other."

These men saw clearly the results of state-sponsored religion. They had observed *"the tragedy of the old world practice of religious persecution being transplanted into the soil of the new world."*[1]

They were aware that the charters given by the English crown to the American colonies gave them authority to establish official religion (assumed to be the Church of England, to which all would be required by force of law to submit and support. In response to this situation, they elected to all government control over religion by denying the government the right to dictate on matters of religion and to guarantee to all the freedom of religion and conscience.

In 1779, during the Revolutionary War, the General Assembly of the fledgling nation removed all penalties against freedom of religion. In 1785, the nation's leaders adopted a bill for religious freedom framed by Jefferson. Then, with the adoption of the Bill of Rights in 1791, freedom of faith and non-interference by government was guaranteed.

RELIGIOUS FREEDOM THE BAROMETER OF CIVILIZATION

The development of the United States in 235 years as a republic is unparalleled in history. This has been due, in part

---

1. Tolle, *Religious Freedom*, 8.

at least, by the liberties guaranteed in our Constitution, not the least of which is freedom of religion.

"Studies tend to show conclusively that throughout history religious freedom has been the barometer of civilization; that in all lands, throughout all times, countries have attained highest prosperity and well-being in exact proportion to their observance of religious freedom."[2]

CHURCH-STATE UNION DISASTROUS

On the contrary, as Tolle points out,

"The evils of church-state union, with the denial of liberty to those who disagree with the established religion, have always been disastrous to the morality and good order of society."[3]

Consider the official state Catholic Church and her Inquisition. Consider the lax morals in the Russian Orthodox Church, joined with the equally immoral and oppressive Czars, which at least in part precipitated the rise of Soviet Communism, which hated all religion. Consider the hundreds of millions of dollars paid by the Catholic Church in lawsuits against its priests for sexual molestation. Consider lands in which Islamic Shari'ah law rules and how all other religions are repressed, or even outlawed and their practitioners severely punished.

State churches have been the ally of tyranny and social oppression. It has tolerated and even encouraged fierce, intolerant and obstructive impulses in which they reign; that

---

2. Dawson, *Separate*, 126.
3. Ibid., 8–9.

is, until they get in the way of the ideology and agenda of some government. Lenin announced,

> "We demand the complete separation of the church from the state in order to combat religious darkness with a purely ideological, and exclusively ideological weapon, our printed and oral propaganda."[4]

FREEDOM OF RELIGION STILL TOLERATED, BUT INFRINGED UPON

Where does our nation stand today on religious freedom? Remember that the First Amendment reads that

"Congress shall make no law respecting an establishment of religion, or prohibiting the free exercise thereof..."

That wording has been the subject of much debate and many judicial decisions. It was meant to protect the citizens from ever having an official religion, such as they had experienced back in England. It forever prohibited Congress from establishing a state religion, or prohibiting the free exercise of religion by the citizens.

Over the years this statement has really been turned upside-down. Now it means that there must be an absolute separation, at all levels, between church and state. In practical terms, it has been construed to prohibit any encroachment on the government by religion. The "free exercise of religion" is no longer being protected. On the contrary, in various realms of activity, religion is limited in its expression—all on the grounds that such expression is "unconstitutional."

---

4. Lenin, *Selected Works*, 664.

In my own city a large church erected an even larger cross on its property. There was a loud outcry about it, the feeling by some being that it infringed on their right not to see any expression of the Christian faith. However, the cross stills stands.

CONCLUSION

Praise the Lord, we still enjoy much religious freedom in this country, although it has been eroded in recent decades by court decisions. Most of the attacks against religion have been against the Christian religion, not against Islam, Buddhism or other faiths. If there is liberty to express our faith, then it should be granted equally to all faiths, with none being singled out for prohibition or punishment.

Freedom of religious conscience is a sacred right, guaranteed by our Constitution. Let us protect and defend it, at all costs. As with all freedoms, if not demanded and exercised, this one will slowly fade away. Only a vibrant faith will withstand the onslaughts in the future on our cherished liberty as a nation.

Chapter 21

Conclusion: In God We Trust... or Do We?

WELL, AFTER digging through hundreds of documents, speeches and reports, we come to the end of this work. My conclusions are several. First, of the making of documents there is no end. Second, much rhetoric, sometimes flowery, went into these documents, speeches and papers. Yet, from them I found golden nuggets of a recurring theme: God has always been present in the thoughts and words of our earliest settlers, our founding fathers and our presidents. God's name or references to Him are carved into our monuments and written above the notes of our national songs.

This doesn't mean that these writers and speakers were paragons of virtue, because some were not. Even Bill Clinton, who slipped into immoral behavior, invoked God in his speeches. However, the intention of our leaders has always been to serve under God's blessings and to invoke Him to grant them on the nation.

Conclusion: In God We Trust... or Do We?

A BASIC BULWARK OF OUR NATION

From the Mayflower Charter on, faith in God has been a basic bulwark of our nation. These pages are only a sampling of this fact. If you have read them, you will certainly agree that faith has figured into our national tapestry.

DESTROYING OUR SPIRITUAL FOUNDATION

Somewhere along the line, however, revisionists have done all they could to destroy this spiritual foundation and expunge references to God or Divine Providence from our history. One of their initial means of stamping out God from our national psyche has been to remove Him from public buildings and schools. They have been quite successful at this, so much so that lesser government and school officials are fearful of even testing their power, timidly agreeing that any reference to God or religion is "unconstitutional." One example of this came to light just recently. A school scheduled a Hallowe'en party. Afterward it was sued on the basis that it had hosted a religious event. And those who initiated the suit won a sizeable settlement. Give me a break! Hallowe'en at one time was primarily pagan, but now it is nothing more than a slightly pagan fun time, especially for children.

Was this event unconstitutional? Of course not! As we have pointed out in this book, nowhere does the Constitution mention Christianity or religion, except in the First Amendment. You remember, do you not, what it says? *"Congress shall make no law respecting an establishment of religion, or prohibiting the free exercise thereof..."*

This amendment deals only with Congress, not with the courts; not even the Supreme Court. Congress cannot decree a particular religious faith, nor can it interfere with the exercise of faith.

PROHIBITION AGAINST GOVERNMENT MEDDLING IN RELIGION

Understanding from this amendment that government is not to impose religion upon our people or prohibit its expression, how then have we come to this constant chorus that religious expression is prohibited in governmental, civil and educational circles? This notion has not come from Congress, but from the courts—from court precedents or case laws, beginning only in 1947. How often Circuit Courts of Appeal or even the Supreme Court, strike down any attempt at "invading" the public realm with religion. How often they have limited the "free expression" of Christian faith. How often they have been the ones who have been unconstitutional in their decisions that the Ten Commandments cannot be displayed at a courthouse or in a school. Do you remember what we said and portrayed earlier about reproductions of Moses and the Ten Commandments in the "high cathedral of jurisprudence," the Supreme Court Building? Again, "sauce for the goose . . ."

FUROR OVER TEN COMMANDMENTS IN PUBLIC VIEW

Lawrence Kudlow, writing in "God Belongs in Temples of Government," says this:

"The Ten Commandments are literally chiseled into the American way of life. But there is a campaign going on that would rid this country of any and all religious references. This is part of the ongoing culture war that would stop religious expression in politics and the public square, even though we remain the most religious of all the major industrial countries. Fortunately, brave people like State Atty. Gen. Greg Abbott, who recently argued the Texas position in Van Orden v. Perry before the Supremes, want to keep it that way.

"Religion has always been central to our national identity. Religious references do not violate the First Amendment, which was never intended to bar all religious expression or discussion from national discourse. James Madison himself, the author of the First Amendment, was sworn in with his left hand on the Bible. So was George Washington, and, I believe, every President since.

"The Ten Commandments provide the very foundation of our nation's legal code. They also make up the basis of the moral values that thankfully guide us in our everyday lives."[1]

Yet again, as of February 2010, the Supreme Court has refused to hear a case in Oklahoma dealing with the presence of the Ten Commandments on the grounds of a local courthouse. This means that a Court of Appeals decision stands that the presence of this monument is unconstitutional.

Ben Rast notes that, "The United States is a nation founded on Christian beliefs and principles. Some would have you believe otherwise, but mentions of Almighty God were ubiquitous in the writings of our founding fathers. Today, Christianity is under attack as never before, and even in the

1. Kudlow, "God," 12.

U.S. Christians are being marginalized. There is a huge insurgency of humanism, paganism and New Age thought that fights expressions of our Christian faith at every turn."[2]

REAPING THE RESULTS

What has happened to public school students since the accumulated court decisions against any kind of prayer, Bible reading and the presence of the Ten Commandments in public schools, coupled with a watering-down of faith in families? In the past decade

- SAT scores in Math and Verbal skills are down 10 percent
- Teen suicide is up 450 percent
- Child abuse is up 2,300 percent
- Use of illegal drugs is up 6,000 percent
- Criminal arrests of teens are up 150 percent
- Number of teenage divorces are up 350 percent
- Births by unmarried girls are up 500 percent

(These figures are based on census statistics from the year 2000.)

While we are considering statistics, our prisons nationwide are overloaded, not only with murderers, but also with child molesters, family abusers, thieves, drug dealers and extortionists. When God is removed from our consciousness, what remains is the condition found in Judges 21:25: *"In those days Israel had no king; everyone did as he*

2. Rast, "Striving."

saw fit" (NIV). In our days we have relegated our King Jesus to near oblivion. As a result, we have a country in which, more and more, our citizens expect special privileges: You deserve this. Get what you deserve. You have a right to have what everyone else has. You have a right to receive as much government aid as possible. And if we don't get what we "deserve," some of us cheat and steal to get it. Gone, evidently, are the days when John Kennedy said, *"Ask not what your country can do for you. Ask what you can do for your country."* Or, even better, ask what you can do for your Lord.

What do these shocking statistics and our welfare-state mentality tell us? That with God no longer figuring significantly in the lives of teenagers in their home life and school, their moral fiber is coming unraveled, just as predicted by many of our Founding Fathers. Here is what Washington said about morality without religion:

"And let us with caution indulge the supposition that morality can be maintained without religion . . . Reason and experience both forbid us to expect that national morality can prevail in exclusion of religious principles . . ."

General Douglas MacArthur once said,

"History fails to record a single precedent in which nations subject to moral decay have not passed into political and economic decline."

I'm afraid that is happening to our country today. Rampant immorality is shaking our Christian heritage, and our culture is slipping into a chaotic, frenzied godlessness.[3]

---

3. See Rast, "Striving."

THE INIQUITY QUOTA OF NATIONS

Howard E. Vos reminds us clearly that nations have "iniquity quotas," that is, a time when their immorality has become ripe for punishment. He cites the case of Sodom and Gomorrah as examples. He quotes Genesis 15:16, in which the Lord told Abraham that *"the sin of the Amorites had not yet reached its full measure."* In other words, its "iniquity quota." Haas npt yet been filled. He concludes by wondering *"about the iniquity quotas of modern cities and countries."*[4] With our contemporary preoccupation with political correctness and permissiveness, along with a pervading sense of personal entitlement, how far away is our own country from becoming ripe for punishment? Remember, "Blessed is the land [only] whose God is the Lord."

AN OFFICIAL "HIGH WALL OF SEPARATION"?

May I remind you again that the oft-quoted letter by Thomas Jefferson about "a high wall of separation between church and state" is neither law nor in the Constitution? This same Jefferson invoked God publicly. If there really were a high wall of separation between church and state, why did he include the mention of God in his addresses and other writings? Why have presidents from Washington to Obama invoked God's blessings in their presidential oath of office, inaugural speeches and other addresses? Indeed, why are Christmas wreaths placed on the crosses at Arlington Cemetery and at the Tomb of the Unknowns? And why are there even crosses marking graves at Arlington?

---

4. Vos, *Bible Manners and Customs*, 118–19.

Retrospect and Final Word: In God Do We Really Trust(?)

IF "IN GOD WE TRUST" offends Buddhists, Hindus, Muslims, Wiccans and other groups, as some Web Page entries affirm, so be it! Our nation was not founded basically by followers of any of these religions. It was founded by people whose religious orientation was Christian, or at least whose orientation was faith in God. I pray that the material presented in this book proves that fact. Why, after about 235 years of our history, do we want to alter it, to make it more acceptable for those who have a different religious orientation or world view? Our founding was what it was and it remains anchored, perhaps more loosely now, but still anchored, in faith in one Supreme God. Entertainer and religious figure Pat Boone observed on this point,

"*America is emphatically a Christian nation, and has been from its inception! Seventy percent of her citizens identify themselves as Christian. The Declaration of Independence and our Constitution were framed, written and ratified by Christians.*"[1]

Very true, Pat. Your statement is a good summary to close this book, with one clarifying additional statement: Our nation is Christian in her roots and moral bearings (or at least used to be), but she is not a theocracy, in the sense

---

1. From an e-mail sent to the author, March 29, 2011.

of a government of clerics and their religion administering the government. Our nation is a republic, which guarantees religious freedom to all, but one we pray that will always be built on a foundation of Christian values. *In God we must trust or we as a nation will not long survive.*

John F. Wilson, a professor at Princeton University and director of its Project on Church and State, says this:

"When the founding Fathers proposed in the minimalist attention to religion was not its wholesale segregation from government . . . Nor did they propose that the federal regime should take over (and thus make use of) churches . . . Rather, they proposed that religious institutions should lie beyond the authority or competence of government. Religious activities were a part of the social and cultural life of the new nation which the distinctly limited federal government had no mandate to supervise or to depend upon."[2]

Beyond the authority or competence of government! This was the mentality of men who had watched the overpowering political influence of the established church in England, and they wanted no part of it. I don't believe it ever entered their minds that individuals and organizations in our nation should be restricted in their religious expression, nor that they should not invoke God in their governmental deliberations. How far our nation has fallen from that lofty view of church and state!

May this volume help in some way to draw us back to truly trusting in God at all levels of government and society, before it is too late to find our way back.

---

2. Wilson, *Religion & Politics*, 85.

Appendix

Were Our Founding Fathers Deists?

Some who attempt to undermine the Christian foundation for our nation claim that the Founding Fathers (or at least, many of them) were Deists. That is, they believed in God on a purely rational basis without reliance on revelation or authority—in a God who wound up the universe and then left it to its own devices, taking no part in its functioning beyond original creation. Deists would refer to God as the Almighty Being, Supreme Author of the Universe, Supreme Agent, Providence, the Great Governor of the World, and other such more or less abstract expressions. This was a popular belief in the Age of Enlightenment, especially the seventeenth and eighteenth centuries.

Were our Founding Fathers—Washington, Franklin, John Adams, Jefferson and others—really Deists and not Christians? Some were moderate Deists, but apparently held, judging by their writings, some of the basic tenets of Christianity. These, promulgated by Edward, Lord of Cherbury, England, were:

- That God exists.
- That He ought to be worshiped.
- That living a virtuous life is the basic way of doing so.

- That one can repent of his or her sins.
- That there is life after death.[1]

To this list I would add their belief that God is not responsible for disasters or horrible human behavior.

Author Gary Scott Smith notes that "... those who accepted Deism relished its focus on Christ's moral teaching rather than on theological speculation, personal conversion and religious experience, which orthodox Christianity emphasized."[2]

Many beliefs of Deists can be readily accepted by Christians, so what made the Deists unique? They did not believe in the divinity of Jesus, nor in miracles, nor in the Divine inspiration of Scripture, even though they cited it at times. Jefferson went through his Bible and cut out the miracles and some other acts and teachings of Jesus.

Yet, Franklin, perhaps the most Deist of all, had this to say about God and civil government:

"You desire to know something of my religion ... Here is my creed. I believe in one God, Creator of the Universe. That he governs by his Providence. That he ought to be worshipped. That the most acceptable service we render to him is doing good to his other children. That the soul of man is immortal, and will be treated with justice in another life respecting his conduct in this.

"I shall only add, respecting myself, that having experienced the good of that Being in conducting me prosperously through a long life, I have no doubt of its continuance in the

---

1. Breig, "Deism," 32, citing David Holmes, a professor of religious studies at William and Mary College.
2. Smith, *Faith and Presidency*.

next, though without the smallest conceit of meriting such goodness."

CONCLUSION

In the final analysis, there were Deist expressions in our national documents from that era. Yet, our Founding Fathers who had Deist leanings did not altogether abandon Christianity. Franklin summarized something of his faith in this statement:

"I've lived, sir, a long time, and the longer I live, the more convincing proofs I see that God governs in the affairs of men. If a sparrow cannot fall to the ground without His notice, is it probable that an empire can rise without His aid? We've been assured in the sacred writings that unless the Lord builds the house, they labor in vain that build it. I firmly believe this, and I also believe that with His concurring aid, we shall succeed in this political building no better than the builders of Babel."

Thomas Buckley, SJ, professor of American religious history at the Jesuit School of Theology, Berkeley, Calif., prefers to call them "rationalistic Christians," believing that Jefferson, on his worst days, was not a true Deist.[3] There may have been a relatively few Deists in colonial and revolutionary America, but these few had some impact on the early development of our nation, joining other more traditional believers to frame our freedoms' operating manual.

Don M. Powers summed it up nicely in these words: "Despite the efforts of academia and others to color the founders as Deists and Atheists, the historical records show

3. Breig, "Deism," 34.

quite accurately, and with great clarity and specificity [that] most all founders were Christian . . . The founders truly believed in and lived their individual trust in God."[4]

---

4. Powers, "Founding Fathers," A4.

Bibliography

America's Christian Heritage. Video. Ft. Lauderdale, FL: Center for Reclaiming America, n.d.

Barton, David. *Original Intent: The Courts, the Constitution, and Religion*. Aledo, Texas: Wallbuilder, 2010.

Benen, Steven. "One nation, easily divisible? National hysteria erupts when federal appeals court ejects 'under God' from pledge of allegiance." *Church & State* 55:7 (2002).

Boone, Pat. "The President Without a Country." 2010. No pages. Online: www.snopes.com/politics/soapbox/patboone.asp.

Branham, Robert James. "God Save the___! American National Songs and National Identities, 1760–1798." *Quarterly Journal of Speech* 85:1 (1999).

Breig, James. "Deism: One Nation Under a Clockwork God." *Colonial Williamsburg* 31:2 (spring 2009).

Bruns, Roger A. "Known but to God." *American History* 31:5 (1996) 38–42, 73.

Church, Forest *So Help Me, God: The Founding Fathers and the First Great Battle over Church and State*. Boston: Haoughton Mifflin Harcourt, 2007.

Clement, Edith Brown. "Public Displays Of Affection . . . For God: Religious Monuments After *Mccreary* And *Van Orden*." *Harvard Journal of Law & Public Policy* 32.1 (2009) 231–60.

Collins, Ace. *Songs sung red, white, and blue: the stories behind America's best-loved patriotic songs*. New York: HarperResource, 2003.

Dawson, Joseph Martin. *Separate Church and State Now*. New York: R. R. Smith, 1948.

Devorah, Carrie. *God in the Temples of Government II*, Human Events Online, 2003.

Dunn, Gregory. *God and Empire: Some Theological Reflections on the State of the Union*. Editorial, Ashbrook Center for Public Affairs. Ashbrook, Ohio, Ashbrook University, 2003.

Eidsmoe, John. *Christianity and the Constitution: The Faith of Our Founding Fathers*. Grand Rapids, MI.: Baker, 1991.

Federer, William J. *America's God and Country: Encyclopedia of Quotations*. Coppell, TX: Fame, 1994.

Fisher, Louis, and Nada Mourtada-Sabbah. "Adopting 'In God we trust' as the U.S. national motto." *Journal of Church and State* 44:4 (2002) 671–92.

Gaustad, Edwin S. *A documentary History of Religion in America to the Civil War*. Grand Rapids, MI: Eerdmans, 1993.

Gingrich, Newt. *Rediscovering God in America: Reflections on the Role of Faith in our History and Future*. Nashville: Integrity, 2006.

Goode, Stephen "Presidential Pep Talks." *Insight on the News*, Vol 12, No, 6. February 12, 1996, page 22.

Grant, George. *The Patriot's Handbook: A Citizenship Primer for a New Generation of Americans*. Elkton, MD: Highland, 1996.

Holmes, David L. *The Faiths of our Founding Fathers*. New York: Oxford University Press, 2006.

Jefferson, Thomas. *Jefferson Writings*. Princeton, N.J.: Princeton University Press, 1950.

Kudlow, Lawrence. "God Belongs in Temples of Government." *Human Events* 61:9 (2005).

La Fontaine, Charles V. "God and nation in selected US presidential inaugural addresses, 1789–1945: Part One." *Journal of Church and State* 18:1 (1976) 39–60.

Lenin, Vladimir. *Selected Works, XI.*, n.d.

Leudtke, Luther S., ed. *Making America: The Society and Culture of the United States*. Chapel Hill, NC: University of North Carolina, 1992.

Mac, Tobey, and Michael Tate. *Under God*. Bloomington, MN: Bethany House, 2004.

Mayflower Compact, November 11, 1520. The National Center for Public Policy Research's Archive of Historical Documents, Washington, DC.

McDowell, Stephen, and Mark Beliles. *In God We Trust Tour Guide*. Charlottesville, VA: Providence Foundation, n.d.

McMillon, Lynn. "Dialogue: A conversation with Colt McCoy." *The Christian Chronicle* (October 2009) 22.

Meacham, John. *American Gospel: God, the Founding Fathers, and the Making of a Nation*. New York: Random House, 2007.

Newman, Paul S., ed. *In God We Trust: America's Heritage of Faith*. Norwalk, CT: C. R. Gibson, 1974.

Powers, Don. "No Freedom without Religion." *The Edmond (Okla.) Sun*, 10 July 2010, A4).

———. "Founding Fathers Delivered Belief in God into Constitution." *The Edmond (Okla.) Sun*, 24 July 2010, A4.

Prather, William Lambdin. Speech to graduating seniors, Texas State University (now University of Texas), The University of Texas Record, 1905, Volume 6, p. 158, 159.

Rast, Ben. "Striving for John Adams' Utopia." *Contender Ministries*, 20 May 2002.

Reagan, Ronald. Speech at Reunion Arena, Dallas, 1984. www.themoralliberal.com.

Religious tolerance.org, July 1997.

Robinson, B. A. "The U.S. National Mottoes: Their History and Constitutionality." *Ontario Consultants on Religious Tolerance* (14 October 2008). No pages. Online: http://www.religioustolerance.org/nat_mott.htm.

———. *The Silencing of God: The Dismantling of America's Christian Heritage*. Video. Montgomery, AL: wvbs.org, n.d..

Robison, James. Reflections on Fort Hood Massacre. From wordsoflife.org, message e-mailed 09-16-09.

Rogers, Jay. Published May 2008. www.forerunner.com/statesman/twoviews.

Schwarz, Ted. *Coins as living history*. Georgetown, CN, Arco Books, 1976.

Shogan, Colleen J. *The Contemporary Presidency: The Sixth Year Curse*. Article first published online: Feb. 8, 2006, Wiley Blackwell.

Smith, Gary Scott. *Faith and the Presidency: From George Washington to George W. Bush*. Oxford: Oxford University Press, 2006.

Tolle, James. *Religious Freedom*. San Fernando, CA: Tolle, 1958.

Unruh, Bob. "Now, God banished from *Washington Monument*." *WorldNetDaily* (26 October 2007). No pages. Online: http://www.wnd.com/?pageId=44214.

———. "Ten Commandments stunner: Feds lying at Supreme Court." *WorldNetDaily* (14 November 2006). No pages. Online: http://www.wnd.com/?pageId=38823.

Vos, Howard E. *New Illustrated Bible Manners and Customs*. Nashville: Thomas Nelson, 1999.

Wills, Gary. *Inventing America: Jefferson's Declaration of Independence*. New York: Vantage, 1979.

Wake Up America, Inc. *Our True Heritage*. 2001. No pages. Online: wakeupamericainc.com.

Washington, George. *Daily Sacrifice*. From William J. Johnson, *George Washington, The Christian*. (New York: The Abingdon Press, 1919).

Wieseltier, Leon. "Washington Diarist: God Again." *New Republic* 232:10 (21 March 2005).

Wilson, John F. *Religion & American Politics from the Colonial Period to the 1980s*. Oxford: Oxford University Press, 1990.

Yoder, Frank, from a paper in a series by the Joan B. Kroc Institute for International Peace Studies, Notre Dame Univesity, South Bend, Indiana , 2011).

www.ingramcontent.com/pod-product-compliance
Lightning Source LLC
Chambersburg PA
CBHW051100160426
43193CB00010B/1259